SENSATIONAL
After 60

SENSATIONAL
After
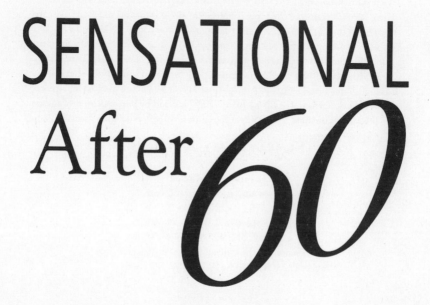

Shirley W. Mitchell

WHITAKER
HOUSE

SENSATIONAL AFTER 60

Shirley W. Mitchell
www.sensationalafter60.com

ISBN: 978-1-60374-747-9
eBook ISBN: 978-1-60374-748-6
Printed in the United States of America
© 2005, 2013 by Shirley W. Mitchell

Whitaker House
1030 Hunt Valley Circle
New Kensington, PA 15068
www.whitakerhouse.com

Library of Congress Cataloging-in-Publication Data (pending)

1 2 3 4 5 6 7 8 9 10 11 ШJ 20 19 18 17 16 15 14 13

DEDICATION

To the most elegant woman I have ever met—
my mother, Willie Todd.

CONTENTS

PREFACE

I wrote *Sensational After 60* from my heart to encourage, inform, impassion, and influence maturing women. Never before in the history of the world has there been a better time to be 60! The wave of the future offers a new perspective to women in their 60s. They are feeling younger and healthier, though growing older, and getting better while aging. This book will help equip them to keep Father Time at bay.

I will not pretend that life never disappoints; after six decades of living in a broken world, we all have experienced pain and heartbreak, broken relationships, and diminishing health. We all have lost dreams and have had to take a detour. Sometimes, reality forces us to adjust our expectations, especially as we age. *Sensational After 60* will help you to see the positive side of aging. This book is for women who dare to accept and anticipate change with a royal attitude and who work at their life from the inside out, fine-tuning their health and looking for joy, while living each day to the fullest.

Sensational After 60 women have the strength of tempered steel and the sweet gentleness of a bride. They are not imprisoned in the past, nor do they refuse to live in the present. Nor do they fear the future; rather, they use each moment as an opportunity to learn, grow, and become increasingly all that they were designed to be. *Sensational After 60* helps women to understand and prepare for what's ahead—to embrace and enjoy the upcoming journey.

HOW TO USE THIS BOOK

Sensational After 60 is designed for women who are approaching their sixth decade or are already in it. The questions for reflection and application at the end of each chapter, along with the Scriptures for meditation (called "Longevity Promises"), make it a perfect tool to use in small groups, Red Hat Society meetings, support groups, and Sunday school classes. Traveling with companions toward sensational aging makes an adventure out of the inevitable, providing invaluable support, laughter, and friendship during the journey.

CHAPTER 1

APPROACHING SENSATIONAL

"We don't grow older, we grow riper."
Pablo Picasso, 1881–1973

"[The righteous] will still yield fruit in old age;
they shall be full of sap and very green, to declare that
the LORD is upright; He is my rock, and there is no
unrighteousness in Him."
—Psalm 92:14–15

A candy company packaged jelly beans in a plastic champagne bottle with a label affixed to the top of the bottle that read, "How Sweet It Is." The colorful advertisement on the front of the bottle yelled, "If things get better with age...you're approaching magnificent!"

I bought that bottle of jelly beans. It now sits on my desk (and has been refilled several times), as a reminder that, though the world tells us otherwise, we can get better with age. We are approaching magnificent, interesting, unique, and sensational years. Though we may fight against the stereotypes of aging, along with poor habits, ingrained lies, and negative role models from our past and present, all of us women still dream of aging sensationally. In *Sensational After 60*, we will search out how to do that!

A sensational 60-something woman has an aura of excitement about her, and those around her can sense her zeal.

— • ● • —

S—Spiritually sparkling

E—Energetic

N—Not negative

S—Smiling

A—Artistic

T—Talented

I—Intelligent

O—Optimal

N—Nubile

A—Attractive

L—Loving

— • ● • —

SQUEAL WITH ZEAL

The aging race is a crowded track! The National Institute on Aging projects that, by 2040, 87 million Americans will be over 65; by 2080, it estimates that there will be 5 million centenarians.[1] Imagine how the world would be if every woman who turned 60 were characterized by zeal!

The aging race is a crowded track! Dr. Ken Dychtwald said that "by 2040, the National Institute of Aging projects that 87 million Americans will be over 65. By 2080, there are expected to be 5 million centenarians."[2] Imagine how the world would be if every woman who turned 60 was characterized by zeal!

Scripture tell us that our Lord was *"clad with zeal as a cloak"* (Isaiah 59:17 KJV). *Merriam-Webster's 11th Collegiate Dictionary* defines *zeal* as "eagerness and ardent interest in pursuit of something." Picture presidential candidates on the campaign trail. They always display eagerness, ardor, fervor, enthusiasm, devotion, passion, verve, and spirit. What an example for us as we approach the second half of our life.

Imagine your 60-year-old life clad with a cloak of zeal. Americans are starting to view older people in a new way. Aging is not what it used to be. The second half of life has become, for many, a time of creativity—not a time to finish the story but to write entirely new chapters. The age limit on physical and mental fitness is expanding. Many older people are heroes well past their 60s.

A CENTENARY HERO

Only a hero could step out on the balcony of Buckingham Palace and receive a thunderous applause from tens of thousands of people. And so it was when the British people celebrated their royal centenary, Queen Elizabeth, the Queen Mother, who was born August 4, 1900. Citizens roared their approval as she appeared, frail but regal in her blue silk dress. Her softness was misleading—a chiffon covering for a tough world leader.

When King Edward VIII abdicated the throne in 1936, Queen Elizabeth described her ascension as "an intolerable honor." Her poise during World War II secured her a permanent position in the hearts of her people. She and her husband, King George VI, refused to leave London during the bombing. When Buckingham Palace suffered a direct hit in September 1940, the queen told reporters, "It allows the royal family to relate to the devastated East End of London." Her sympathy and compassion for the citizens garnered her many loyal fans, as did the common interests she shared with them—good food, horse racing, music (in particular, Sir Noël Coward and Cole Porter), and late-night parties. The Queen Mother was praised for being the glue that held the royal family together.

Her grandson Prince Charles hailed her as "indestructible." Well into her ninth decade, she was still attending over 100 political and other engagements each year. How fitting, then, were the hooplas and hurrahs surrounding the 100-year-old Queen Mom as she rode in an open carriage that day through the flag-draped avenue of the Mall. Imagine the celebration as the royal carriage made its stately procession, preceded by a military band in red tunics and a cavalry unit dressed in silver breastplates and plumed hats.

The Queen Mother epitomized zip, zeal, vigor, and energy—four qualities that provide a rhythm for the song of successful aging. These characteristics are hot commodities for sensational-after-60 women who are looking forward to their own centennial celebration.

The queen's qualities challenge us to live well, to "cloak" ourselves with zeal for the second half of our lives.

MAKE YOUR YEARS COUNT; DON'T COUNT YOUR YEARS

An example of a sensational woman is the country music legend Loretta Webb, born on April 14, 1932, in Butcher Hollow, Kentucky. Loretta married Oliver "Mooney" Lynn as a young teenager and stayed with him until his death in 1996.

Life had taken her through many hard times—difficult marriage in the early years, three children by the age of 19, the drowning and death of her son Jack, and the death of her husband of 48 years. She is prevailing, however, as she continues pursuing her many passions and gifts. Loretta celebrates her family, who add purpose and energy to her life, help her to manage her career and her property, and accompany her on her travels.

She was elected to the Country Music Hall of Fame in 1988 at age 56. In 2002, Loretta published her second memoir, the transparent *Still Woman Enough*, and moved into a new home on a several-thousand-acre working dude ranch. In 2004, she won top artist and also album of the year for *Lear Rose* at the third Americana Music Honors and Awards in Nashville. Loretta Lynn was inducted into New York City's Songwriters Hall of Fame in 2008, at the age of 76. Her most recent album, *Coal Miner's Daughter: A Tribute to Loretta Lynn*, was released in 2010. Loretta is evidently "still woman enough"—even at age 80.

Aside from her present fame, many people do not know much about the shy young woman who first started singing and playing the guitar after her husband, "Doo," bought her a $17 Harmony guitar from Sears and Roebuck, instructing her to learn how to sing and play so that she might add to the family's income. Years of practice paid off. She is still illuminating the stage with her dazzling smile—that radiant look brought on by experience. She ignites the audience's spirit when she belts out her vulnerable, gritty country songs. She clearly makes her years count, instead of counting her years.

Loretta Lynn continues to grow and stretch beyond her comfort zone. She could have surrendered her future and her calling during the hard knocks of life; she could have acquiesced to the "younger is better" mentality. However, this vibrant woman continues to strive toward her best self, mending family fences that were harmed during her years of touring, as she stretches toward the next adventure life has for her.

Loretta Lynn exemplifies zeal, energy, and excitement. All of these qualities, combined, fit the definition of *sensational*.

EVERYTHING OLD IS NEW AGAIN

Dr. Henry Blackaby, author of the best-selling book *Experiencing God*, said that being 65-years-old is "one of the greatest times to experience more of God than you've ever experienced! You're freer to follow God without anyone else stopping you. You're not on anyone else's agenda but God's. Your most productive walk with the Lord is ahead of you, not behind you. Go beyond your comfort zone and let God use you through your whole lifetime."[3]

To grow and stretch, one must be bold and venture into the unknown, leaving behind the comfortable safety and sameness of life, as one has defined it. I stepped out of my comfort zone in 2000 when I decided to participate in the Ms. Senior Alabama Pageant.

My goal, as I stepped inside the well-lit arena, was to learn all the colors and facets of my personality. Maybe a facet or two needed polished. I desired to become more interesting, to make a new friend, to open a new window or door—maybe even a whole new life. On the day I entered the pageant, I wrote in my diary, "I feel energized. I feel empowered."

Ms. Senior Alabama, Inc., is a nonprofit organization dedicated to enriching the lives of older women. Each year, the organization conducts a search in Alabama to locate the most outstanding women 60 years of age and older. The goal of the pageant is to recognize women who are over 60 as important members of society who have many years left to contribute to their communities and country.

"Everything Old Is New Again" was the theme for the over-60 pageant that year, and the participants proved the truthfulness of that motto. Each woman's beauty, talent, and wisdom sparkled on the superbly decorated stage, demonstrating the splendor of aging well.

Spend Your Time and Talent Wisely

The year I participated in the pageant, Ms. Gayle Hester of Gadsden, Alabama, was crowned Ms. Senior Alabama. She was the first woman softball umpire in Etowah County, Alabama. In addition, as an all-star softball player, she had been nominated for the Etowah County Sports Hall of Fame. Ms. Hester had also worked as a receptionist at a cerebral palsy center, as a monitor for a security company, and as an herbalist and salesperson for The Herb Shop. After winning Ms. Senior Alabama, she went on to participate in the National Ms. Senior America Pageant, finishing as second runner-up.

Now that she is retired, Ms. Hester volunteers her time to breast cancer patients (being a cancer survivor herself), as well as to victims of domestic abuse. This dedicated woman belongs to the East Gadsden Baptist Singles, the Classic Ladies Club, the Spice of Life Club, and the Golden Age Club. She is also a Special Olympics "hugger." She is full of energy as she ages well.

Find Your Philosophy of Life

For one of the events in the 2000 Ms. Senior Alabama Pageant, each contestant had to dress in an evening gown, appear onstage, and share her personal philosophy of life with the audience. These gems of wisdom were offered to the listeners, to be fashioned into a sparkling piece of jewelry for them to wear during the second half of life.

My own gem of wisdom was centered on my faith. "With God at the core of my life, I believe in positive aging," I said.

"Surfing the age wave into the new millennium, I will age with good health, power, style, and zeal."

What is your philosophy of life for the second half of life? Where do you find meaning and purpose for your aging years? Write it down on paper. This philosophy of life will help you determine your priorities as you age. Many senior women who demonstrate vitality, talent, and high energy in their latter years do so as a result of some undergirding purpose.

Step Out of Your Comfort Zone

The stage director coordinated quite a fabulous production. For the "talent" component, we formed a chorus line, each of us dressed to represent a specific decade. I was assigned the 1950s. Singing and dancing in a poodle skirt and oxford shoes certainly pushed me out of my comfort zone. It also tested my coordination, my musical skills, and my ability to perform synchronized choreography. It was exhilarating!

What better time than our 60s and beyond to step out of our comfort zone and embrace new experiences.

Smile as You Step Forward with Optimism

In the contest, I happily received the "Most Stunning Smile" award. I learned that a smile is a natural face-lift. We can all benefit from a face-lift, and this one is painless, noninvasive, and free!

Men and women alike are considered "over the hill" on their 40th birthday. It is certainly true that, for most people, age 40 marks the beginning of many physical changes. But it is also the age when women should start questioning and discarding myths about aging in order to develop a more positive, uplifting attitude.

Participating in the Ms. Senior Alabama pageant gave me more of an appreciation for the years I had already lived and the years I had yet to live. It provided me with animation in new areas of my life.

As I was returning home from the pageant, I passed two antique cars, one bright orange, the other blue and white. They had been polished until they shone like new; I assumed that they were en route to a show of some sort. What struck me was that those shiny "old" cars looked just as stylish as the white 2000 Lexus following them—a wonderful example that young isn't necessarily better!

PAINT YOUR AGING PICTURE WITH PRAYER

Stanislaw Jerzy Lec once said, "Youth is the gift of nature, but age is a work of art." If age is a work of art, we can all learn to be better artists. Faith in a living God, who loves us extravagantly, will add bright, living colors to our picture of age.

USA Today ran a front-page article entitled "For Seniors, Prayer Good for Body as Well as Soul," which read,

> The devout have long believed that prayer helps gain admission to the hereafter. But the study suggests that regular prayer, Bible study, or meditation, may have important benefits in the here and now.
>
> Harold Koenig and researchers at the Duke University Medical Center studied 4,000 Christian men and women age 65 and older from 1986 to 1992. The study published in the *Journal of Gerontology* found that seniors who rarely or never prayed had a 50 percent greater risk of dying early. Proof that fairly healthy seniors who regularly study the Bible, pray, and assemble at God's house, can add years to their lives and life to their years.[4]

Spend Time with God

My friend Kathleen Fackelmann exemplifies a harmony of body and soul—physical and spiritual health. Having just turned 60, she pays attention to her body and its symptoms, brings them to God in prayer, and invites Him to show her how to care for herself. When she splurges on a massage, she silently thanks God for the blessings of her body—the years of carrying her, the years of ministry it enabled her to do—and invites Him to restore tired muscles, giving her the energy to live out her calling.

She makes time in her schedule for daily prayer, journaling, and listening to God. The last time I saw her was in a group setting. As a group of our friends climbed up a long flight of stairs, she was the least winded of us all. She said, "This is going to change. I'm going to continue getting in shape." Her determination is fueled by the relationship she has with God, which she cultivates by meeting with Him on a daily basis.

Serve Others

Another one of my role models, Pearl Dychtwald, is not just adding years to her life as she ages; she is also filling it with fun and service to others. After reading *Fabulous After 50*, she wrote to me, saying,

> *Fabulous After 50* is the perfect book for me, as I will be celebrating my seventh-seventh birthday next month. I am happy, in my senior years, to be sharing whatever skills I have learned in my younger years. I volunteer and teach tap dance to a many women in my complex. They love it, and I love it. I take them out to entertain others

at nursing homes, and it becomes a very happy occasion for the elders who live there.[5]

I hope that when I reach 77, I, too, will consider those in nursing homes as my "elders"!

Boost Your Energy

Here are four basic practices that will help women in their 60s boost their energy levels, keeping them young and active:

1. Practice good health habits—the "trump card" of aging well.

2. Keep exercising; it provides fuel for aging.

3. Maintain enthusiasm (which literally means "God inside") about life.

4. Take control of your heart and attitude.

Guard Against Energy Zappers

Look out for these energy zappers, which often cause women to feel sluggish and depressed:

- Boredom
- Poor health
- Lack of exercise
- Lack of sleep
- Stress
- Poor diet
- Lack of anything to anticipate
- Shallow relationships
- Lack of purpose
- Negligent soul care

Women over 60 must steer clear of these energy zappers so that they can maintain a positive approach to day-to-day life. This is the lifestyle that enables women to maintain optimal health—physically, spiritually, and mentally—allowing them to live longer and better.

COUNTRY LEGEND LIVING SENSATIONALLY AFTER 60

Faith and energy whet our appetites for adventure. Women who approach life as an adventure don't grow older—they grow sensational. Minnie Pearl mastered sensational living. She was indeed a real "pearl." Her straw hat may have been worth only $1, but her enthusiasm and attitude were priceless.

She died at age 83, and I still miss turning on the television to her greeting: "How-dee! I'm just so proud to be here." She filled her life—and the lives of others—with faith and humor.

I first met Minnie Pearl at a prayer luncheon in Guntersville, Alabama, in 1971. She autographed my copy of her cookbook, *Minnie Pearl Cooks*, with the words "Happy Cooking!" I remember her telling the ladies at the luncheon that her philosophy was, "Brighten the corner where you are!" She always said, "Laughter is a drug, and I'm totally addicted."

The next time I met Minnie Pearl was when my second book, *Spiritual Sparks for Busy Women*, was published, in 1982. This Grand Ole Opry star interviewed me on her *Noon Show*, live on WSM-TV, in Nashville, Tennessee. She breezed into the studio, looking very sophisticated with a bright yellow suit, high-heeled shoes, and her hair swept into an updo. When she entered, the studio seemed to glow with the sunshine of her upbeat attitude. The audience erupted with laughter at her wit. Her positive spirit and love of life were contagious.

As she interviewed me on air, she held up a copy of my book and read from its pages: "The light of Jesus shines through a woman and makes her sparkle. Her life will shine forth the many facets of Jesus just as a cut gem reflects beautiful color in all directions." Then she exploded with enthusiasm: "Every one of you should go to your favorite bookstore right now and buy this book."

Minnie Pearl's sophistication and down-to-earth character, her warmth and humor, her dignity and charm, broke down the barriers of many women's hearts. Born Sarah Ophelia Colley in Centerville, Tennessee, Minnie Pearl rose to fame wearing a dime-store hat with a dangling price tag from it. Her rise to fame was due to her star role in the popular TV show *Hee Haw*. In 1975, she was inducted into the Country Music Hall of Fame.

The belle of Grinder's Switch, Tennessee, stepped out of her comfort zone when she stepped into this new role as a home-spun comedian. Her famous and inimitable greeting was free from artifice, giving her access to people's hearts. There she stood, on stage in her best dress, telling everybody how proud she was to be there, and she'd forgotten to take the price tag off her hat.

Minnie Pearl felt that the price tag on her hat symbolized human frailty. The way she embraced her frailty with laughter—refusing to take herself too seriously—and honored that frailty in others sets an example for all those who long to be sensational after 60.

APPROACHING MAGNIFICENT

As we forge ahead into the second half of life, we have to decide: Are we going to be sensational or stagnant? Are we going to move toward magnificence or mediocrity? Are we going to walk purposefully or aimlessly? Thankfully, the commodities of life experience, faith in a living God, determination to step out of our comfort zone, a cloak of zeal, and the remembrance that everything old is new again will distinguish us as sensational-after-60 women.

• ● •

"Remember the past, imagine the future,
celebrate the present."
—Shirley W. Mitchell's Diary

• ● •

QUESTIONS FOR REFLECTION AND APPLICATION

1. List three ways that you can make your years count, instead of counting your years.

2. How can you make your life "squeal with zeal"?

3. Brainstorm ways in which you can share your experiences, wisdom, and skills with others.

SEVEN SIMPLE SECRETS FOR BEING SENSATIONAL AFTER 60

1. Redefine your life.

2. Step out of your comfort zone.

3. Celebrate every day. Choose to focus on one gift each day.

4. Write down your philosophy of life. You're already on your way when you've put it into words!

5. Pray!

6. Share with others the skills you have learned.

7. Keep your zeal alive!

LONGEVITY PROMISE

"He hath made everything beautiful in his time."
—Ecclesiastes 3:11 (KJV)

Endnotes

1. Dr. Ken Dychtwald, *The Age Wave* (Los Angeles, CA: Jeremy P. Tarcher, Inc., 1989), 8.

2. "Life," *USA Today* (29 September 2004): 1.

3. Bonnie Shepherd, "Still Experiencing God: An Interview with Henry Blackaby," *LifeWise Magazine* (December 2000–January 2001): 13.

4. Kathleen Fackelmann, "For Seniors, Prayer Good for Body as Well as Soul," *USA Today* (31 July 2000): 1.

5. Letter from Pearl Dychtwald. Used by permission.

CHAPTER 2

WHAT TO EXPECT IN THE "60s" SEASON

"I am not a has-been. I'm a will-be."[1]
—Lauren Bacall

"Let the favor of the Lord our God be upon us;
and do confirm for us the work of our hands;
yes, confirm the work of our hands."
—Psalm 90:17

Aging during what Ken Dychtwald calls the "Age Wave" is a high-seas adventure. Sixty years of experience and strength buoy us up into a position where we can welcome this new decade with open arms.

Women in their 60s should be delighted to explore the "sea" of change—and the deep-sea treasures—ahead of them. As our responsibilities toward our families become fewer and fewer, we find ourselves with the time and energy to pursue our passions and reach toward a creative peak. With retirement in view, we may even start anticipating new activities that we have always dreamed about doing. Many exciting opportunities emerge in the sixth decade of life.

Yes, I said "exciting." This decade brings sweeping change, perhaps more change than any other season of life—except, perhaps, the teenage years. In our 60s, our perspective on life changes from what it was 40 years ago, when we thought, *I have my whole life ahead of me.*

What changes can we expect in this next decade?

A SEASON OF CHANGE

Riding the high seas of adventure in the sixth decade of life may start with retirement and the questions that come with this type of change: Will I relocate? Will my finances be tight? What will my health care and insurance look like? Will the system into which I've invested still be available to me?

Additionally, with changes in family setups and jobs, we face identity issues: Who am I without a paycheck or the other rewards of having a job? Who am I without a family and/or a spouse to care for? We must reinvent ourselves as the ways in which we invest our time and talents, on both people and pursuits, change. There will be times when we experience loneliness, and we may find ourselves compelled to seek reconciliation and renewed relationship with those whom we have long ignored, due to various circumstances.

Issues that women face in their 60s often revolve around retirement, relocation, relationships, reconciliation, and regrets. The one thing these all have in common is that they call for reinvention, refocus, and renewal. The key to a fulfilling life is having a heart for God, a heart for abundant life, and a heart for renewal. In their book *The Sacred Romance,* Brent Curtis and John Eldredge remind us that Jesus of Nazareth invites us "to a life of beauty, intimacy, and adventure."[2] Aging with these qualities in mind can empower us to meet the new challenges and changes we will face in this decade. Faith needs to be the filter through which we see our future.

STORM AT SEA

Are the storms of aging rousing sky-high waves from the sea of life—waves that threaten to capsize you? Such was the case for my friend and mentor, Kathleen Garrett, who related the following incident to me.

My petite, charming, high school economics teacher and I were having lunch at a local restaurant, The Food Basket. As I looked at her across the table, I could tell that she had been struggling with something, and I guessed that it was related to her health.

"How are you feeling?" I asked. "You look great!"

As we ate, she shared her secret with me. "My doctor at Mayo Clinic gave me a unique prescription," she said, her eyes twinkling.

I must have looked puzzled, for she quickly added, "He advised me to enhance the quality of my life by getting out of bed each morning and saying, 'Make each day a holiday and each minute a banquet!'"

This sounded like a principle of renewal to me. We overcome our trials by letting God renew us day by day. As we choose our heart's focus, He calms the raging waves. Consider these words of the apostle Paul:

Therefore we do not lose heart. Though outwardly we are wasting away, yet inwardly we are being renewed day by day. For our light and momentary troubles are achieving for us an eternal glory that far outweighs them all. So we fix our eyes not on what is seen, but on what is unseen. For what is seen is temporary, but what is unseen is eternal.

(2 Corinthians 4:16–18 NIV)

A new day is dawning! Let your heart be encouraged. When the storms of life threaten your peace and security—when they slap against the sides of your boat, splashing into your life—do not waver. Pray for "sea legs" and hold on to the Captain's wheel! Jesus is the One who quiets the sea, who commands the storm to calm. Stand firm in Him and in His power! During our golden "graying" years, we must move from life to life; we must keep watch for the sunrise, even in the darkest night; and we must wait for the calm that comes after the storm.

Reverend Grady Nutt, who played the "Prime Minister of Humor" on the show *Hee Haw*, spoke a few years ago at a banquet in Cullman, Alabama. The title of his discussion was "Live Every Day like It Would Be Your Last." He preached and practiced my friend's "holiday and banquet" advice. That night, he was killed in a plane crash. God took Reverend Nutt to his heavenly home.

The only certainty our future holds is the promise that we will live in heaven and share a glorious future with the King. Life on this earth is as fragile as a flower. Darkness and despair will cause it to wilt; the sunshine of joy will make it bloom. Though the nighttime is dark, the sun rises each morning with healing in its wings. (See Psalm 30:5.)

"A FRESH NEW DAY"
By Shirley W. Mitchell

The early morning sunlight
spreads its rays across the sky

like great golden fingers,
making my spirits fly high!

The brightness of God's sunlight
cheers my soul and warms my bones.
What a magnificent creation,
God's great beauty to behold!

God says to me in the stillness,
"Feed My lambs with great delight.
In a world that's filled with darkness,
I want you to be My sunlight."

SHINING AS STARS

God empowers His aging children to shine as stars, even in times of change. Many of the changes that we experience in our 60s revolve around our relationships. After years of raising a family, many of us find ourselves living in empty, silent homes. We are no longer surrounded by the cheerful voices of our children and their friends; no more does constant activity engage our senses. Growing older sometimes involves adjusting to new settings— quiet homes after years of being filled with love and laughter.

As we move into the empty nest of midlife, it's important to keep a sense of humor. In her numerous books and newspaper columns, American humorist Erma Bombeck encouraged the maturing population to keep their humor alive. Even while she was on the waiting list for a kidney transplant, undergoing dialysis four times a day, she wrote hilarious columns. She was so busy living that she did not have time to fear dying.

Erma poked fun at aging and the complications it brings. In one column, she wrote about how it seemed that her adult children always came to visit only when she had cooked enough food for just one person. "I cook enough spaghetti to feed Sicily, and no one shows. I nuke a small piece of leftover pizza for dinner, and they fly in from out of state."

Erma Bombeck received her kidney transplant, only to die of complications from the procedure. But her legacy is one of levity and humor. Lives that are filled with laughter help to elevate our spirits and to rise above the darkness of change.

CREATIVE PEAKS

If you find yourself, in this season of life, staring into a large window of time after the children have left and your career is waning, try to redirect your gaze. This is your time. Decide to follow actress Lauren Bacall's advice—focus on your future life instead of your past life. Refuse to be a "has-been." Become a "will-be." Do not allow society's standards of beauty and youth to define or limit you. The sixth decade may be the time when you will reach your creative peak.

Diane Sawyer, former host of ABC's *Good Morning America* and current anchor of *ABC World News*, said, "We should be incubating something new—a second career, a more passionate hobby for the later years—just to make sure that we're stretching and growing and not just repeating ourselves."[3]

At 60-something, I felt that I was climbing a mountain to my creative peak. My fourth book, *Fabulous After 50*, gave me an opportunity to step out of my comfort zone as I traveled around the country to promote it. I learned to speak in front of television cameras, to articulate information over the phone, and to broadcast over the radio. I am still honing my skills as I continue to speak and travel. Constant challenges jump-start my creativity and keep me charged.

All of us are creative in our own way. And how could we not be, as children of the Creator God, who plants creativity inside each one of us? With creativity as our birthright, we can continue to cultivate the special gifts He has given us. "And I [the Lord] *have filled* [My children] *with the spirit of God, in wisdom, and in understanding, and in knowledge, and in all manner of workmanship*" (Exodus 31:3 KJV).

When we cultivate the gifts mentioned in that passage, they benefit not only us but others, as well. In order for this to happen, however, we must give of what God has planted inside us. If not, we will wither on the vine and miss our blessing, while also depriving others of their blessing.

A great Christian artist by the name of William Hallmark painted a life-size portrait of me. In the painting, he captured the feeling I had inside my heart at the time. This has been a great blessing to me, and it came during a season when I was burdened by the stress of midlife. Mr. Hallmark saw my heart with the eyes of an artist and painted it with competent strokes. If he had not pursued his God-given talent, I would have missed out on an enormous blessing.

Well into her 80s, my mother blessed people daily by baking delicious cakes and distributing them to friends, family, and other people who were sick or hurting. Accompanying every cake was a hefty portion of hope from a woman who always refused to shut down in old age but remained determined to use her creativity and gifts to bless others.

My aunt is a very skilled quilter, using various scraps of fabric—of all shapes and sizes—to create a masterpiece. She enjoys the party atmosphere and rich conversation that accompany gatherings with other quilters. They sit around their quilting frames and sew dainty stitches while spinning funny stories and sharing family memories. They interweave work and play to create beautiful works of art. Quilters give these exquisite products as wedding gifts, which are used as warm covers on beds or wall hangings, to make a room extraordinary.

Talents and gifts, regardless of size or shape, multiply when we use them and share them in grace. Are you cheating someone out of a blessing by not using your gifts? What are your gifts, and what do you need to do to incorporate them into your daily life? More education? More training? A friend to hold you accountable?

Now is a great time to explore the possibilities, dream of your potential, and get more education or training so that you can take advantage of new opportunities that will boost you to your creative peak.

LATER YEARS AND LIFELONG LEARNING

If your 60-something life seems to be in "pause" mode, then you are a prime candidate for more education. The mind needs as much exercise as the physical body. Most institutions of higher education offer evening classes, continuing education classes, and great libraries. Special rates often apply to seniors. The possibilities are endless. Many retirement homes are situated near college campuses, allowing seniors to participate in concerts, lectures, and theater productions—all kinds of mind-engaging enjoyment—as well as to mingle with high-energy young people.

When Lanette and Jim retired, they each enrolled in master's courses at their local community college and completed degrees in subjects that were totally different from the careers they had but had always fascinated them.

Many churches have dynamic education programs for seniors with courses designed to stretch them out of their complacent patterns of living and develop more vibrant minds, hearts, and souls. For example, Dauphin Way Church in Mobile, Alabama, offers ten ongoing senior ministries, including a school of continuing education with more than 25 courses.[4]

Even while working, I never stopped learning. I successfully completed the requirements to become a Christian Leaders, Authors, and Speakers Seminar (C.L.A.S.S.) Communicator. Participating in the C.L.A.S.S. seminar years ago, which featured Littauer, Florence Littauer, and a staff of professional speakers and writers, gave me the skills and confidence to become a better writer and speaker. I still attend the Write-to-Publish Conference each year to learn how to keep my writing and speaking up-to-date.

John Glenn, the first American astronaut to orbit the earth, is a wonderful example of a man who continued learning well into his later years. At age 77, he revisited outer space on the Space Shuttle Discovery Mission to discover the effects of space on the aging body. His courage riveted the nation. In addition to space exploration, John Glenn also enjoyed a career in international business and served 24 years in the U.S. Senate. His life serves as a reminder that life after 60 can be exciting, rewarding, and hopeful. John Glenn continues to be a role model for all those in their 60s who desire to start a new career or to fulfill a dream. It's never too late.

For many aging people, starting a new career is the last thing on their mind. Perhaps you have your retirement funds in order, and your desire is to enjoy life and "smell the roses" by traveling, golfing, volunteering, taking dance lessons, attending a cooking class, or pursuing some other activity.

It is the greatest time in history to be in one's 60s! Within every aging woman is hidden wealth, waiting to be mined, teeming with nuggets of golden greatness! But it isn't enough to merely possess the potential for extraordinary living and

achievement. The nuggets must be mined, brought to the surface, taken through the fires of adversity, and polished into sparkling brilliance.

There are many aging women who have discovered this
untapped gold mine and have torn away the archaic veil, discovering a side to themselves that was hidden for far too long
under a defeatist attitude. But, once they discovered the brilliant vein of potential that runs through this "mine" of aging,
they tapped into it, forging a path toward fulfillment, happiness, health, and satisfaction beyond their wildest dreams.
What a positive difference we can make in the lives of other
seniors, especially as we give other women a reason to hope for
their own exciting, productive futures! The opportunities are
limitless!

SOLO AT 60

Many women in their 60s find themselves alone. Singleness
is a reality that many older women must face after living through
separation, divorce, or the death of a spouse or child. The U.S.
Census Bureau reports that more than 36 percent of women
between the ages of 60 and 64 live alone, whether they have
never married or have lost a spouse through death, separation,
divorce, or absence. This figure jumps 10 percent in the next ten
years of life.[5]

Solo at 60 became a firsthand experience for me, when, after
38 years of marriage, I went through a divorce that darkened my
world. The change has been difficult and painful but not insur-
mountable. Though it took time and effort, I grieved, forgave
my ex-husband, and eventually picked up the pieces of my new,
single life. A new career, a new path to travel, and, most of all, a
new outlook, carved a new route for me to follow.

As in every season of life, we can choose to rise above our circumstances—to become victors rather than victims. During my devotional time each morning, I sip coffee from a mug that reads, "New Beginnings—In life, what sometimes appears to be the end is really a new beginning."

To combat the loneliness, I surround myself with friends who challenge me, remind me of my calling and gifts, and make me laugh. I don't run from solitude. Instead, I seek God first, then my friends and colleagues. Only when we pursue relationships in this order does life begin to balance itself.

EMBRACING THE SIXTH DECADE

Scientific advancements in the past few decades have redefined the meaning of aging. Now we know that we must use it, or we will lose it. We must train our brains that aging does not have to be negative.

Moses serves as a good mentor for all of us. He lived a sensational life and held on to hope well past the time when others would have given up. When Moses started approaching his seventh decade, God called him away from his career as a shepherd and gave him a new vocation: overseeing nearly 1.5 million slaves and being part of the plan to set them free. It was quite the journey. *"Although Moses was one hundred and twenty years old when he died, his eye was not dim, nor his vigor abated"* (Deuteronomy 34:7).

Imagine—120 years old! And many who are reading this book are only in their 60s. As Fred Astaire once said, "Old age is like everything else. To make a success of it, you've got to start young."

Journalist and author Judith Viorst shared her own thoughts on the aging process in the following poem:

"IF ONLY"

If only shopping at Saks counted as exercise.
If only aggravation made me thin.
If only there was a pill I could take for grace
    under pressure and upper-arm definition.
If only I lost as adorably as I win.

If only having insomnia gave me courage.
If only eating chocolate made me smart.
If only there was a cloth that washed off lipstick,
    mascara, eyeliner, blush, and wrinkles.
If only my breasts and my waist were farther apart.

If only going to movies lowered cholesterol.
If only constipation made me rich.
If only there was a shot that would immunize me
    against impatience and feeling guilty.
If only I laughed as easily as I....

If only French fried potatoes helped me remember.
If only they sometimes also helped me forget.
If only one morning I'd leap out of bed feeling ready
    and willing and eager to welcome old age.
But not yet.
Not yet.
Not yet.
But not quite yet.[6]

• ● •

*"When God plants a seed in your mind and
a passion in your heart, go for it! Experience a lifetime of
loving, living, learning."*
—Shirley W. Mitchell's Diary

• ● •

QUESTIONS FOR REFLECTION AND APPLICATION

1. What specific challenges might you experience in the sixth decade? What excites you? What frightens you?

2. Take a look at the seven "revitalizers" listed below. Which r words apply to you in this season of life?

3. How do you feel about creativity in this stage of life? What seeds might you sow in your heart that will bud in your soul in this decade?

SEVEN 60-SOMETHING REVITALIZERS

1. Retire

2. Reinvent

3. Reconcile

4. Reinvest

5. Relocate

6. Recharge

7. Renew

LONGEVITY PROMISE

"I will fulfill the number of your days."
—Exodus 23:26

Endnotes

1. Bonnie Miller Rubin, *Fifty on Fifty: Wisdom, Inspiration, and Reflections on Women's Lives Well Lived* (New York: Warner Books, 1998), 129.

2. Brent Curtis and John Eldredge, *The Sacred Romance: Draw in Closer to the Heart of God* (Nashville, TN: Thomas Nelson, Inc., 1997), 7.

3. Rubin, *Fifty on Fifty*, 124.

4. *Interpreter* (July–August 2003): 11.

5. U.S. Bureau of the Census, *Current Population Survey* (March 1999).

6. Slightly revised from Judith Viorst's poem "If Only," printed in *Suddenly Sixty and Other Shocks of Later Life* (NY: Simon & Schuster, 2000), 79.

CHAPTER 3

FIERCELY FEMININE

*"We are told to let our light shine, and if it does,
we won't need to tell anybody it does.
Lighthouses don't fire cannons to call attention to
their shining—they just shine."*
—D. L. Moody

"In him was life; and the life was the light of men."
—John 1:4

Eating at a restaurant last week, I observed a beautiful older woman who was escorted to a seat by her handsome companion. Her shoulder-length salt-and-pepper hair shined beautifully, reinforcing an article I had recently read that said gray hair was in fashion. This is great news! Gray hair is fashionable for the fiercely feminine 60-year-old. I recently saw a picture of the gorgeous actress Helen Mirren, whose coiffure is completely gray. On the other hand, there are also many high-profile executives who dye their hair in order to achieve a younger look. That's great, too! Whether we keep our hair gray or dye it, we can still be grand in our sixth decade.

I am thrilled as I observe the women celebrating their 60th year—women who are groomed to a high gloss and who walk with a posture of grandeur, wearing stylish clothes and stilettos. They are fiercely feminine. There is an air of confidence about this new army of women who are making a difference in the world with honor, courage, and integrity. They shine as lights in this world of darkness.

Before the cross, all people are equal. For this reason, women who accept Jesus Christ as their personal Savior have a level playing ground on which to enjoy the journey of life. We are connected to an omnipotent (all-powerful), omniscient (all-knowing), and omnipresent (present everywhere) God. How awesome is that?

Now is the perfect time to embrace the fact that life never ends, as well as to anticipate a future with Christ in the great big family of God. Moving beyond the ordinary to the extraordinary through Jesus Christ will catapult you into God's supernatural power. When you keep your spirit healthy through a relationship with God, your light will shine into all the world.

PURSUE YOUR PASSION

God created you with a unique genetic makeup—no one else has your DNA. Your talents and passions are programmed into your DNA by your heavenly Father. If your desire is to be 100 percent alive in your 60s, then you must follow the God-given desires of your heart. When you pursue God's calling, engaging your gifts and passions, you will enjoy being 60-something. If you have a dream, don't let it die. Go for it!

Passion is an intense emotion, a feeling of unusual excitement and enthusiasm. A passion for Christ, a loved one, an art, a profession, or a cause, such as helping those in need, stimulates and enhances life. During your 60s, your passions may differ from those of your earlier years. Only you know the deep passions of your heart. Have the courage, through Jesus Christ, to pursue your passions with gusto. When you do this, life after 60 will explode with new energy and charisma.

STEP INTO YOUR AUTHENTICITY

Be real, and own your age with pride. Your strength, ambition, and faith have blessed you with long life. And your genuineness will shine the light of Jesus on your aging path, all the way to your eternal home in heaven. Share the wisdom that you've gained over the years with the people in your circle of life. When many women reach their 60s, they have a sharpened sense of discernment. Sharing this gift will allow them to be an encouragement to younger people.

STEP INTO YOUR FEMININITY

As you age, never stop enjoying your femininity! One way to do this is to read through the Song of Songs, the most sensual book of the Bible. Here's an excerpt to whet your appetite:

How beautiful are your feet in sandals, O prince's daughter! The curves of your hips are like jewels, the work of the hands of an artist. Your navel is like a round goblet which never lacks mixed wine; your belly is like a heap of wheat fenced about with lilies. Your two breasts are like two fawns, twins of a gazelle. Your neck is like a tower of ivory, your eyes like the pools in Heshbon by the gate of Bath-rabbim; your nose is like the tower of Lebanon, which faces toward Damascus. Your head crowns you like Carmel, and the flowing locks of your head are like purple threads; the king is captivated by your tresses. How beautiful and how delightful you are, my love, with all your charms! Your stature is like a palm tree, and your breasts are like its clusters. I said, "I will climb the palm tree, I will take hold of its fruit stalks." Oh, may your breasts be like clusters of the vine, and the fragrance of your breath like apples, and your mouth like the best wine! It goes down smoothly for my beloved, flowing gently through the lips of those who fall asleep. I am my beloved's, and his desire is for me.   (Song of Songs 7:1–10)

No matter their age, God's women are always feminine!

STEP INTO YOUR FREEDOM

Free is a word that aptly describes many sensational-after-60 women. Many women in their 60s have the freedom to enjoy the lives that they have built for themselves. I know a Christian couple in their 60s who have raised a beautiful family, have retired from successful life work, and are still very much in love. They enjoy traveling together, as well as doing all the things they had no time for in their previous years.

On the other hand, some grandparents take on the responsibility of raising grandchildren due to divorce or illness in the family. Although this can be very difficult, the rewards can be great! I have also witnessed many sensational 60-year-old women who, after working toward their goal for many years, are experiencing a professional high, often accompanied by monetary rewards. This time in life can be very gratifying.

In 2012, U.S. Secretary of State Hillary Rodham Clinton made *Time* magazine's list of the 100 most influential women in the world. Robert Gates, former U.S. Secretary of Defense, and current chancellor of the College of William and Mary, wrote about her in the magazine: "Secretary Clinton has been thoughtful and tough-minded about where and how the U.S. should engage its prestige, its resources and its men and women in the field, both civilian and military. She is an idealistic realist and a superb Secretary of State and has well served the President and our country."[1] At 65 years of age, Hillary Clinton continues to be highly influential. We have the same potential!

You may find yourself single at 60, as I did. But that does not have to limit your potential. Again, I started my 60th year by participating in the Ms. Senior Alabama Pageant. This choice motivated me to undergo a complete makeover. Winning an award for my smile boosted my confidence. I stretched out of my comfort zone further than I thought possible by traveling to Washington, D.C., and getting involved in President George W. Bush's presidential campaign. This experience was riveting, as I had the opportunity to meet many enthusiastic people.

Being an author, speaker, and radio talk show host has kept me mentally, physically, and socially active. At age 62, I published *Fabulous After 50*. In order to promote the book, I had to keep up my motivation to stay "moving and grooving." As long as a woman remains confident in who she is (made in the image of Jesus), it hardly matters the number of years she has lived. The majesty and splendor of the presence of the Holy Spirit in her life will make her shine like a Christmas tree!

Dr. Ken Dychtwald said it well:

Historically, Americans led "linear" lives because so many only lived into their 50s and 60s. Today, a new model of life is emerging. People want to distribute the longevity bonus. They are going back to school at 40 and coming back from illness to run a marathon at 80. They are beginning as late bloomers and hitting their stride in later years. The new model of life means aging isn't an isolated zone in "Seniorville." We are thinking about people as beginning again and again.

If you find yourself in a place of new beginnings, whether you are starting a different profession, getting married again, or traveling to uncharted territory, step out in confidence! Be creative, artistic, and up-to-date. Seek professional help and always look your best, because looking good helps you feel good, no matter your situation.

AWAKEN TO THE ART OF LIFE

Get out of your head and into the art of life. We can take in the beauty of artistic grandeur everywhere we look. This morning, I sat on my patio and watched the sun rise. I felt fully alive and awake as the brilliant rays of the sun popped over the horizon. The sounds of birds chirping filled my soul with joy. The rays of sun warmed my skin, and the shimmering dewdrops lifted my spirit. And the beautiful, fluffy white clouds that floated in the azure sky almost made me cry with joy. As the sun broke through the clouds, I thanked God for the moment of heightened awareness and appreciation of His universe.

How often are we caught up in the cares of life and the limits of time, so much so that we miss out on sacred moments such as these! As we focus on God's magnificent universe, we begin to better appreciate the gift of life. Truly, *"The heavens declare the glory of God; the skies proclaim the work of his hands"* (Psalm 19:1 NIV). The art of life expands to heaven, earth, and sea.

SHINE AS A LIGHT

Jesus said,

You are the light of the world. A city on a hill cannot be hidden. Neither do people light a lamp and put it under a bowl. Instead they put it on its stand, and it gives light to everyone in the house. In the same way, let your light shine before men, that they may see your good deeds and praise your Father in heaven. (Matthew 5:14–16 NIV)

Furthermore, Paul said in Ephesians 5:8, *"You were formerly darkness, but now you are light in the Lord; walk as children of light."* The light of Christ penetrates the darkness, and His light is in you. Therefore, you should shed the light of Christ as you age. That love will prevail over dark situations, because God is love. Be strong enough to give it away, bringing hope and light to everyone. A candle loses nothing by lighting another candle. So, as a fiercely feminine woman, carry a light that ignites others!

QUESTIONS FOR REFLECTION AND APPLICATION

1. Take the time to think about how the cross of Christ makes all people equal, despite their age. How does this make you feel?

2. What talents and passions has God imbedded in your DNA? How can you apply them or bring them back to life?

3. How can you use your gifts to encourage and benefit others, including the younger generations?

SEVEN SIMPLE CHARACTERISTICS OF THE FIERCELY FEMININE WOMAN

1. She walks in the light of Christ, knowing that age is irrelevant to experiencing the power of the cross.

2. She fulfills old passions, as well as discovers new ones.

3. She walks with authenticity.

4. She steps out of her comfort zone and experiences new things.

5. She is confident in her own skin, knowing that she is a masterpiece of God.

6. She takes the time to enjoy the beauty around her.

7. She is a light to the younger generations.

LONGEVITY PROMISE

"Even to your old age, I shall be the same, and even to your graying years I shall bear you! I have done it, and I shall carry you; and I shall bear you, and I shall deliver you."
—Isaiah 46:4

Endnote

1. Robert Gates, "The World's 100 Most Influential People: 2012," *Time* (18 April 2012), http://www.time.com/time/specials/packages/article/0,28804,2111975_2111976_2111951,00.html.

CHAPTER 4

PASSION + PERSISTENCE + PREVAILING = PIZZAZZ

"There is a real magic in enthusiasm. It spells the difference between mediocrity and accomplishment...it gives warmth and good feeling to all your personal relationships."[1]
—Norman Vincent Peale, age 63

"We exult in hope of the glory of God. And not only this, but we also exult in our tribulations, knowing that tribulation brings about perseverance; and perseverance, proven character; and proven character, hope; and hope does not disappoint, because the love of God has been poured out within our hearts."
—Romans 5:2–5

Oliver Wendell Holmes once lamented, "Some people die with the music still in them." That's a crime! Take the time today to listen to the music of your soul, to the melody that has played in your heart at various times throughout your life. Don't let the music die for fear of failure or lack of education. Psalm 46:10 says, *"Be still, and know that I am God"* (NIV). In the stillness, invite God to open your heart and your ears to hear the song that He is whispering there.

The music in my soul is to encourage aging women to sing the song within *their* souls, and to use the Word to encourage seniors to make the latter half of their lives the better half.

Perhaps this dream comes from my enormous love for life—life thrills me, and it is inseparable from my faith. I love Jesus' words in John 10:10: *"The thief comes only to steal, and kill, and destroy; I came that they might have life, and might have it abundantly."* I will not allow the thief of aging to steal my joy and zest for life; instead, I will depend on Jesus' life-giving abundance.

By walking in the richness and totality of life, we can become a generation of people who belie their age. Although gravity and additional years act as natural bulldozers at times—sending our spirits crashing to the ground—our passions, persistence, and prevailing spirits can bring back the joy in life!

PURSUING YOUR PASSION

Do you have a dream? What is your passion? Go for it! Now is the time. Life becomes a passionate adventure when we dare to dream—when we defy society's stereotypes of aging. A dream can evolve into a remarkable life for the 60-plus woman. Rev up your dreams! Dream power can shoot you to the stars!

Prepare for Pursuit

In 1970, my love of life prompted me to write my first article, which was published as a feature article with my picture in Stonecroft Ministries' magazine, *Progress.* Not only was it the feature article, they also put my picture on the cover. Being published spurred my passion for sharing my faith through the written word. I set up my first office—my writing space—in the corner of our den at home.

Following your passion requires preparation. I decided to prepare for this dream by attending a Write-to-Publish conference that was held at Moody Bible Institute in Chicago. Upon returning home after the conference, I began writing my first book, *The Beauty of Being God's Woman*, on a manual Royal typewriter. I completed the manuscript with two school-age children living their noisy, chaotic lives around me.

Maintain Childlike Wonder

Whether one is 16 or 60, a sense of wonder makes the gift of years a precious jewel. And the giants of life need not steal this wonder from us! Michael Yaconelli writes in his book *Dangerous Wonder*,

> We have forgotten what it is like to stand speechless in the presence of Jesus, hearts beating wildly, staggered and stunned by what God is doing in our world. The obstacles are intimidating, but they need not dictate our lives. We can rediscover the childlike attribute of our faith called dangerous wonder....You can still experience a volatile mix of astonishment and terror, awe and risk, amazement and fear, adventure and exhilaration, tears and laughter, passion and anticipation, daring and enchantment.[2]

One way to restore this passion for life, this sense of childlike wonder, is to persist in spending time with God. I love to begin each day in quiet intimacy with my heavenly Father. If the activities of the morning rush in and steal this time, I make a special effort to get away from the noise in the afternoon or evening so that I can isolate myself and commune with the living God. During my devotional time, I invite God to speak to me through His love letter—the Bible. I listen as He speaks to my heart and my mind. I talk to Him through prayer, like a little girl would talk to a loving Father.

Times of intimacy with God balance my busy life and help me to order my priorities and goals. I also keep a diary, which becomes more valuable as the years progress. I even purchased a fireproof safe in which to store these writings. I am glad I have persevered through the busyness of life and set time aside to spend with God. My passion to be in the presence of God, as well as the persistence to keep it a top priority, has added pizzazz to my life. I am alive from the inside out!

"TAKE TIME"
Author Unknown

Take time to work—
    it is the price of success.
Take time to think—
    it is the source of power.
Take time to play—
    it is the secret of perpetual youth.
Take time to read—
    it is the fountain of wisdom.
Take time to be friendly—
    it is the road to happiness.
Take time to dream—
    it is hitching your wagon to a star.
Take time to love and be loved—
    it is the privilege of redeemed people.
Take time to look around—
    it is the music of the soul.
Take time for God—
    it is life's only lasting investment.[3]

PURSUING PERSISTENCE

My manuscript spent a fair amount of time sitting on publishers' desks until a local firm, Strode Publishers in Huntsville, Alabama, picked it up and decided to publish it. During the time that the book was going through its second printing, they published my second book, *Spiritual Sparks for Busy Women*. I was ecstatic! And during the time that they were proofing my third book, *The Christian Writer's Desk Diary*, a close friend called me.

"Have you seen the morning news?" she asked.

"No," I said. My heart thudded with fear.

"Strode Publishers burned to the ground last night!"

I was sad and shocked when I heard the news. With their entire warehouse in ashes, Strode Publishers had no choice but to go out of business. I remember lying facedown on the floor and praying to God, "Do You intend for me to stop writing?" After about two weeks, I felt in my spirit that I had to continue writing. The Lord spoke to my heart, "Follow your bliss." I learned that tribulation can produce perseverance, that perseverance proves character, and that passion and persistence can produce hope!

During this period, three women in my prayer group met with me weekly. They prayed a lot for me, and one woman offered her garage apartment for me to use as a writing office.

The apartment was nestled among the tops of pine trees, and I loved the private haven it offered. It was my escape when my children were in school. I escaped from the distractions of "undones" and duties and ringing phones and just wrote. I wrote articles for magazines, as well as a weekly column, Lace over Steel, for a newspaper. It was during this time that God gave me a desire to write a fourth book.

When my friend with the garage apartment moved away, I had to vacate my nest in her wooded yard and search for a new office. My husband made some room for me in his horse barn. In the midst of a stable full of horses, which were frequently trained and groomed for shows, I continued to hone my writing skills by working on the magazine articles and newspaper column.

When the horse barn became an even bigger hub of activity, I boxed up my office supplies and moved to a house trailer that had been vacated by my brother. The embers of my passion and persistence for writing still glowed in my heart.

In 1992, I met Dr. Ken Dychtwald, who planted a seed in my mind during his Age Wave Institute in New York. That seed germinated into my fourth book, *Fabulous After 50*. Fifteen years after my third book had been published and 25 submissions later, I had an opportunity to meet with the publishing team at New Leaf Press in Green Forest, Arkansas. Persistence paid off!

I have now come full circle. My office and computer are back at home, and God has transformed my passion and persistence into pizzazz as I speak around the country, cheering women on as they seek to be fabulous after 50 and beyond—to live sensationally in every season of life.

Never Give Up

Throughout those years, it was a struggle to maintain my vision. Though I was always serious about writing, I often put the manuscript in the drawer between submissions and rejections. A story about Winston Churchill encouraged me as I struggled to remain persistent in reaching my writing goals.

Sir Winston Churchill took three years getting through eighth grade because he had trouble learning English. It seems ironic that, years later, Oxford University asked him to address its commencement exercises. He arrived with his usual props. A cigar, a cane, and a top hat accompanied Churchill wherever he went. As Churchill approached the podium, the crowd rose in appreciative applause. With unmatched dignity, he settled the crowd and stood confident before his admirers. Removing the cigar and carefully placing the top hat on the podium, Churchill gazed at his waiting audience. Authority rang in Churchill's voice as he shouted, "Never give up!" Several seconds passed before he rose to his toes and repeated: "Never give up!" His words thundered in their ears. There was a deafening silence as Churchill reached for his hat and cigar, steadied himself with his cane, and left the platform. His commencement address was finished.[4]

Never give up! That was, no doubt, the shortest and most eloquent commencement address ever given. Those words should echo in our ears, whenever challenges, tribulations, and opportunities come our way.

The threads of passion and persistence sew together life's fabric and envelop tomorrow with hope. Never give up—not even when giants threaten on the horizon.

Study People Who Have Persisted

When we feel unable to persist, and when we have lost our passion, we must look at the lives of others who, by dint of their passion and persistence, have overcome great obstacles.

My grandmother was one such woman. Fannie Esther raised four boys and one girl on a cotton farm. I would help her pick cotton, dragging the pick sack behind me between the rows. Each day, she made our work a competition to see who would pick more pounds. As we lugged our sacks down the rows, I learned not only the value of persistence but also the importance of investing in others. We were great friends.

Fannie Esther was both beautiful and talented. She played the piano at church and nurtured a thriving garden of vegetables and flowers at home. Furthermore, her cooking skills rivaled those of the greatest chef. But, more than that, she loved a scrawny little girl enough to show her how to prevail in the difficult work of a tenant farmer. She was a godly woman of great character.

Sarah Josepha Hale, editor of the *Ladies' Magazine* and *Godey's Lady's Book*, both published in the 1800s, had a unique passion for expressing gratitude and appreciation for the gift of life in America. In her perseverance, she persuaded President Abraham Lincoln to institute a national day of thanksgiving on the fourth Thursday in November. Her passion and persistence equals our pizzazz today as we celebrate Thanksgiving each year with family and friends around a turkey feast.

Helen Keller is one of my favorite heroines who persisted through difficulty:

> Totally deaf and blind, Helen Keller became a famous author and lecturer. Instead of wallowing in grief, Helen Keller lived life fully in spite of her handicaps. She even graduated cum laude from Radcliff College. Helen Keller had perfect perseverance.[5]

Yet another one of my heroines is Corrie ten Boom, who survived the indescribable terror of a Nazi concentration camp. After her release, she continued fighting, along with her family, against anti-Semitism and injustice. She persisted with strong faith—a faith that had been tested and proven by fire—and went on to write *The Hiding Place*. She traveled around the world, telling her story of courage and forgiveness. Countless people have turned their lives over to the God Corrie loved. Her pizzazz changed the world and healed broken hearts after the trauma of World War II.

PREVAILING

The third variable in our formula for pizzazz is having a spirit that prevails. When we add passion, persistence, and a prevailing spirit to our equation for sensational living, the sum is pizzazz!

In an interview for *Parade* magazine, actress Lauren Bacall shared that she followed her dreams and was open to whatever life had in store for her. When her dear friend William Faulkner won the Nobel Prize for literature, he wrote a dedication to her: "To Lauren Bacall, who was not satisfied with just a pretty face, but rather decided to prevail."

Prevailing in the Face of Adversity

A brilliant woman named Esther was not satisfied with a pretty face, either. She used her beauty and her situation as an opportunity for God to redeem an entire nation from genocide. She prevailed over the fear of death, risking both her reputation and her life to overthrow an evil plan. Out of all the Hebrew women of the Bible, Esther shines most brightly. The name Esther is derived from the Persian name Aster, meaning "star." This word implies a star of good fortune, a star of superiority, and a star of joy. Esther certainly earned the accolades associated with her name.

Orphaned as a child, Esther, daughter of Abihail, moved to the city of Shushan and was placed under the guardianship of Mordecai, a relative and palace official. Her original name, Hadassah, was changed to Esther because of her great beauty.

Mordecai developed a deep affection for her and raised her as if she were his own daughter.

When King Xerxes (King Ahasuerus, in some Bible versions) searched for a new wife to replace Queen Vashti, his eyes fell on Esther. Her beautiful, exotic features made her stand out, and her charm and poise made her the king's top choice. It was not long before she was chosen as the next queen.

Early in Esther's reign as queen, Mordecai learned that Haman, a wicked and spiteful ruler, hated the Jews. While occupying a supreme position in King Xerxes' court, he developed a strategy to massacre the Jewish people. Mordecai warned Esther of Haman's plans and asked her to use her position as queen to persuade the king to overturn the death decree.

Esther knew that to approach the king without being summoned first could mean death. Knowing that the king's former wife had been deposed for disobedience must have shaken Esther to the core. But, after three days of prayer and fasting, Esther, a true patriot, sought to prevail and approached the king.

> *Esther put on her royal robes and entered the inner court just beyond the royal hall of the palace, where the king was sitting upon his royal throne. And when he saw Queen Esther standing there in the inner court, he welcomed her, holding out the golden scepter to her. So Esther approached and touched its tip.*
>
> (Esther 5:1–2 TLB)

The king had favor on Esther and honored her request to spare her people. Her courage, along with Mordecai's wisdom, became the means of saving the Jews. She prevailed in a situation that seemed impossible by human standards.

Prevailing in the 60s

We live in a society that puts a lot of stress on external beauty. But Esther's story reminds us that true beauty comes from the inside. What is truly beautiful is having the courage to fight against the world's standards and to choose life.

The world will tell us that a woman's beauty and her usefulness both fade with age. Every time we turn on the TV, Hollywood reminds us that value decreases as wrinkles increase; that how one looks is more important than how one lives. This is why prevailing in this seemingly rigged aging game takes planning.

It may also require us getting politically involved. Imagine the impact that the millions of baby boomers could have on their grandchildren if they showed up at the polls and voted for the future political leaders of America. In the last presidential election, the age group that contributed the most votes was between the ages of 45 to 64 years, followed closely by those who were 65 and older. Like Queen Esther, who prevailed and saved her people from extermination, we, too, can move our country in a powerful, positive direction.

Joyful and tragic experiences alike give us opportunities to prevail. They put the ballast in our boats and the wind in our sails. We need both kinds of experiences to keep us moving through the seas of aging. Helen Keller once said, "We could never learn to be brave and patient, if there was only joy in the world."[6] In times of trial, we must hang on to the memory of the great times in order to feed our soul, so that our souls won't develop "wrinkles" and give to God the place called "wit's end."

The sixth decade is the accumulation of all of the years we have lived. The experiences and wisdom that we have accumulated empower us to take the challenge of a closed door and turn it into an open door of adventure.

Robert Browning captured the passion and power of the midlife years in his poem "Rabbi Ben Ezra":

Grow old along with me!
  The best is yet to be,
the last of life, for which the first was made:
  Our times are in His hand,
Who saith: "A whole I planned,
  youth shows but half,
trust God, see all,
  nor be afraid."

Come! Ride the crest of the wave of aging with me onto the beach of longevity and creative change. The largest group in our society is living in the second half of life with better health and more zeal than any generation before it.

Our calling cards in the sixth decade are passion, persistence, and a prevailing spirit. It takes only a spark to get a fire going. Allow the sparks of passion and persistence to light a fire in your heart to be sensational after 60!

Remember, God Is Greater than the Giants of Aging

Paradoxically, at 60-something, our future seems to be filled with both hope and dread—dread of the giant problems that aging often brings. There are problems concerning independence and dependence, health, loneliness, loss, and so on.

Searching God's Word for courage as I looked toward the future, I gathered strength from the story of Caleb and Joshua. After a 40-day journey in the desert to flee slavery in Egypt, the Israelites arrived at the edge of the Promised Land. Twelve of the tribe leaders were sent out to spy on the land of Canaan.

The men found great walled cities, strong people, and even giants. They also found what God had promised: a land flowing with milk and honey. They brought Moses a cluster of grapes from the Promised Land that was so big, it took two men to transport it.

Ten of the men saw giants and compared themselves to grasshoppers. But Caleb and Joshua focused on the possibilities instead of the problems. They said, "We can!" The difference is that Caleb and Joshua factored the Lord into the equation.

> *Caleb stilled the people before Moses, and said, Let us go up at once, and possess it* [the Promised Land]; *for we are well able to overcome it.*　　　(Numbers 13:30 KJV)

Caleb and Joshua delivered their message with a different spirit. Life with God turns problems into possibilities. On the other hand, the ten men who said "We can't" died of a plague. (See Numbers 14:36–37.) But God doubled the lifespan of Caleb and Joshua and sent them to conquer the land 40 years later.

Courageous Caleb, who conquered the negativity of old age with vigor and faithfulness to God, said,

> *And now, behold, the LORD hath kept me alive, as he said, these forty and five years, even since the LORD spake this word unto Moses, while the children of Israel wandered in the wilderness: and now, lo, I am this day fourscore and five years old. As yet I am as strong this day as I was in the day that Moses sent me: as my strength was then, even so is my strength now, for war, both to go out, and to come in. Now therefore give me this mountain.*　　　(Joshua 14:10–12 KJV)

Sensational women in their 60s are the Calebs and Joshuas who enter the land of aging with courage, surrender to God, vigor, a can-do spirit, and a positive attitude.

We need to say in our hearts, and to shout before the enemies of aging, "Give me this mountain!" God is greater than the giants of aging—poor health, loneliness, financial and relational insecurities, changes brought about by death, separation, divorce, the need to be needed, and lack of passion.

Though these giants may make us feel like grasshoppers, remember that God will give us the courage to possess the Promised Land of aging—a land of abundance, flowing with milk and honey. We need to renew our vantage point on the second half of life and begin anticipating the years ahead. The latter half of life has the potential of becoming the best when we look at the future from our 60-plus vantage point with wisdom, experience, self-knowledge, and a mature faith in God.

Maintaining a Positive Outlook

A key to having a positive attitude is to focus on the opportunities that a challenging situation presents, not the drawbacks and trouble. We must train our brains to see the world positively, and learn the secret of an optimistic outlook. Some perks of positive thinking include (1) higher self-esteem, (2) a healthier immune system, and (3) the energy to make things happen. A positive attitude makes the path to old age full of stepping-stones rather than stumbling blocks.

Another way we can maintain a positive outlook is to take good care of our bodies. It's the little things we do every day that have the biggest impact on how successfully we will age. Establishing healthy habits in our early years makes it likelier that we will carry on with them in our later years.

Listen to your body. Keep your muscles in motion. Plan a time to exercise each day to build your strength and resilience. Be active. Eat a healthy diet to provide fuel for your body. Foster a spirit of faith, hope, and love, which makes life worth living.

Keep the stars in your eyes and hope in your heart. Stay interested, motivated, and involved.

Regardless of the other variables in life, this formula never changes:

Passion + Persistence + Prevailing = Pizzazz!

• ● •

"God planted your passion. Flow with it, power it with vision, activate it with action, enjoy the rewards. Allow lesser priorities to fall by the wayside. Focus."
—Shirley W. Mitchell's Diary

• ● •

QUESTIONS FOR REFLECTION AND APPLICATION

1. Whom do you admire most when it comes to exhibiting passion, persistence, and a prevailing spirit?

2. When have you chosen to persist and prevail in spite of difficulties and no-can-do thinking?

3. What are you passionate about? How will you pursue that passion?

SEVEN EXTRA VARIABLES IN THE AGING FORMULA

1. Enthusiasm
2. Energy
3. Encouragement
4. Exercise
5. Education
6. Eternal thinking
7. Expectancy

THE "P" VARIABLES

1. Passion
2. Persistence
3. Prevailing spirit
4. Priorities
5. Principles
6. Privacy
7. Practice
8. Play
9. Prunes (Ha! Kidding.)
10. Pulse (Okay, okay.)
11. Pizzazz

LONGEVITY PROMISE

"And it shall come to pass afterward,
that I will pour out my spirit upon all flesh...your old men
shall dream dreams, your young men shall see visions:
and also upon the servants and upon the handmaids in
those days will I pour out my spirit."
—Joel 2:28–29 (KJV)

Endnotes

1. Gretchen B. Dianda and Betty J. Hofmayer, *Older and Wiser: 716 Memorable Quotes from Those Who Have Lived the Longest and Seen the Most* (New York: Ballantine Books, 1995), 207.

2. Michael Yaconelli, *Dangerous Wonder: The Adventure of Childlike Faith* (Colorado Springs, CO: NavPress, 1998), 29.

3. Marion Stroud, *The Gift of Years* (New York, NY: Inspirational Press, 1991).

4. Glenn Van Ekeren, *The Speaker's Sourcebook* (Englewood Cliffs, NJ: Simon & Schuster, 1988), 276.

5. Van Ekeren, *Speaker's Sourcebook*, 275.

6. Quoted in the *Atlantic Monthly* (May 1890).

CHAPTER 5

MY DIARY: TURNING 60

*"We are beginning to write another page in history.
Last night, we looked at the past,
how the world was when the second millennium began.
Today, beginning the year 2000, we cannot but question
ourselves about the future—what direction will the great
human family take in this new stage of its history?"*[1]
—Pope John Paul II

*"For through me [the fear of the Lord] your days will be
many, and years will be added to your life."*
—Proverbs 9:11 (NIV)

When the ball in Times Square dropped in New York City, ushering us into the 2000, a new millennium dawned. What an awesome experience it was to step over the threshold of a new millennium. On January 5, 2000, I wrote my pledge for the New Year: "Remember the past, celebrate the present, and imagine the future."

Remembering my past provides me with a foundation that I can build on for the rest of my life. Celebrating the present is an opportunity to live fully in the "now." Imagining the future allows me to enhance my life by setting goals to fulfill later on down the road.

This threefold approach to life—remembering the past, celebrating the present, and imagining the future—gives momentum and balance to our lives. In a world that views aging as a depressing reality, we need to maintain a balanced outlook on life.

As we gain inspiration from our past while expanding our personal dreams for the future, we are filled with magical possibilities in the present. It helps us to fight the battle of the dull, and it keeps us from giving up and succumbing to those pessimistic views of aging that are so prevalent today.

Della Reese, who played the role of Tess on the TV series *Touched by an Angel,* offered a lovely example of how the past can shape the present. She told *Parade* magazine, "Everything that has happened to me has made me the woman I am today. I like that person. I respect her. She's courageous and honest."[2]

We are definitely a product of our past. Not only does our past shape us; it can—despite its hardships—empower us to become all that we were created to be in the future.

DESIGN-A-LIFE

Sometimes, we forget to envision the future—we forget that we have the freedom to design our lives with the Holy Spirit as our director. At age 60, it's time to design the life you want. In his book, *You Can Be President (or Anything Else),* Bob Moore wrote:

Today I am not afraid; I feel confident toward myself and what I can accomplish. I am a president: president of my thoughts, president of my actions, president of my reactions, and president of the quality of my work. I am president of my life.

As president, I am free to carry out any type of administration I wish—good, average, or poor. However, I know that what I give to my administration determines what life gives me in return—not luck or fate. Whatever my action, I can expect the same type of reaction from the world in return.

In the past, I have been like the average person and used only 10 percent of my potential and ability; 90 percent of what I can be and do is still inside me begging to be used!

Today I will handle well all the situations that I face because I will use more of the untapped potential and ability that I possess.

I AM SOMEBODY…I am the PRESIDENT OF MY LIFE. Mine will be a good administration. I have potential! I have ability![3]

I am delighted to share with you some excerpts from my diary—truths and hopes condensed from a year when I wrestled with my past, accepted the gift of the present, and dreamed about and planned for my future.

ENCOURAGING EXCERPTS

January 18, 2000

I listened as president of the University of Montevallo, Robert McChesney, quoted some of political theorist John Schaar's words:

The future is not a result of choices among alternative paths offered by the present, but a place that is created—created first in the mind and will, created next in activity. The future is not some place we are going to, but one we are creating. The paths are not to be found, but made, and the activity of making them changes both the maker and the destination.[4]

Looking back over my years, I find that my own experience affirms this truth. We think it, we determine it, and we do it. The education I had at the University of Montevallo has helped me to make wise choices that have made my life sensational. But before I ever wandered onto that campus or sat at a desk to prepare for my future, I made the most important decision of my life: I chose to invite Jesus Christ into my life, that He might live and rule from the throne of my heart. I was born into the royal family of God. I became a Christian—a child of the King.

Now, 45 years later, that choice continues to shape my future. So, what is my anti-aging secret? It was the choice I made to *"serve the LORD with fear, and rejoice with trembling"* (Psalm 2:11 KJV). Serving the ageless One gives me a focus far beyond the worries of aging—wrinkles, health, income, career, and relationships. This practice (and I do mean practice!) brings tremendous rewards. *"He shall be like a tree planted by the rivers of water, that bringeth forth his fruit in his season; his leaf also shall not wither; and whatsoever he doeth shall prosper"* (Psalm 1:3 KJV). This is an unfailing plan, because God's plan trumps all others. When we align our heart with God's, He guides our choices and produces fruit. Choosing Christ removes all the worry from aging!

Scripture is what helped me transition into my 60s with wisdom, integrity, and energy. The Bible is filled with keys to aging well and living long, and I clung to those as I journeyed on.

January 19, 2000

Judy Ball, managing editor of a newsletter by St. Anthony Messenger Press, wrote about the new millennium:

For me, it is a deeply spiritual moment. This moment in history reminds me that 2,000 years ago, He [Jesus] came to this earth to show us how to live. I certainly hope that the year 2000 will help me deepen my commitment to be a follower.

The Bible, which was my millennium bridge, says in Leviticus 25:11 that *"the fiftieth year shall be a jubilee for you"* (NIV). Wayne Muller wrote in *Forbes* magazine, "The book of Leviticus in the Bible counsels people to set aside every seventh year to observe a Sabbath, a 'year' of rest for the land and the people. Further, it declares every seventh Sabbath year—every 50th year—a year of Jubilee."[5]

Even though this is not my 50th year, I plan to build a year of Jubilee on its principles: rest, renewal, observing God's work in the past, trusting God during His work in the present, and anticipating His work in the future. I have chosen to follow Paul's example in Philippians 3:13–14, where he said, *"...reaching forth unto those things which are before, I press toward the mark for the prize of the high calling of God in Christ Jesus"* (KJV).

And what a prize that is! To honor this year of Jubilee, I will meditate on the Bible day and night. Joshua 1:7–9 (NIV) reads,

Be strong and very courageous. Be careful to obey all the law my servant Moses gave you; do not turn from it to the right or to the left, that you may be successful wherever you go. Do not let this Book of the Law depart from your mouth; meditate on it day and night, so that you may be careful to do everything written in it. Then you will be prosperous and successful. Have I not commanded you? Be strong and courageous. Do not be terrified; do not be discouraged, for the LORD your God will be with you wherever you go.

Praise God for His Word. I do not have to fear the territory of the 60s, because, as I meditate on God's promises, He gives strength, courage, and His presence.

April 24, 2000

Making final preparations for the publishing of *Fabulous After 50*, packing for a vacation in New York City, and feeling connected to God, family, and friends, have made my day an explosion of zeal!

I feel very blessed with life. My prayer is to be like the fine porcelain in my china cabinet—strong, sturdy, beautiful, and transparent. I want to be feminine, sensitive, and smart. I pray that God's zeal and brilliance will spill over the brink of heaven and fill me.

I have a zeal for inviting people into the fullness of life—and people over 60 are ready to live fully! Jesus said, "The fields are white with harvest" (see John 4:35), and, while we may not have white heads like the cotton balls I picked in the South, the autumn of our lives is the time for fullness. Lord, help me to help others enter into that fullness.

May 7, 2000

> *"Every experience God gives us, every person*
> *He puts in our lives, is the perfect preparation for the future*
> *that only He can see."*[6]
> —Corrie ten Boom

Sometimes, God puts people in our lives long before we understand His purpose behind it. In 1992, I flew to Chicago, eager to hone my writing skills at the Write-to-Publish Conference and ready to minister to the large population of aging seniors. In the cafeteria that we ate in at the conference, I met one of my dearest friends, Jane Rubietta. Jane and I shared our dreams and hopes with each other that day and became fast friends.

Photo by John Keith Photography

Jane Rubietta

We have become sisters in Christ—writing, speaking, promoting, and traveling together. We pray for each other often.

Being a member of the royal family of God is an adventure— each encounter with a new person or situation can impact our futures! What an intriguing life!

June 3, 2000

As I read my Bible this morning, I noticed a little note that I had jotted in the margin on April 20, 1992. It read, "Lord, I am casting my net on the right side of the boat. Write *Fabulous After 50* through me and publish it in Your perfection and in Your timing." The passage of Scripture to which my prayer referred to was:

Afterward Jesus appeared again to his disciples, by the Sea of Tiberias. It happened this way: Simon Peter, Thomas (called Didymus), Nathanael from Cana in Galilee, the sons of Zebedee, and two other disciples were together. "I'm going out to fish," Simon Peter told them, and they said, "We'll go with you." So they went out and got into the boat, but that night they caught nothing. Early in the morning, Jesus stood on the shore, but the disciples did not realize that it was Jesus. He called out to them, "Friends, haven't you any fish?" "No," they answered. He said, "Throw your net on the right side of the boat and you will find some." When they did, they were unable to haul the net in because of the large number of fish. (John 21:1–6 NIV)

Aging is a lot like fishing: It is so much harder to do without Jesus filling the nets of our lives. I have felt like those fishermen must have felt after a long night with nothing but empty, sagging nets. But, at the word of the Master, they let down their nets and caught so many fish, they could not pull them over the side of the boat.

So it was with me. My net feels full of fish! After years of manuscript submissions and rejections, I felt like a failure. But, when I had cast my nets into the waters for the right publisher, in God's timing, the manuscript for *Fabulous After 50* was accepted! Praise God!

June 5, 2000

A new day is born! I met God in the morning when I knelt to pray.

Today I read about Paul's experience in prison as he wrote to the Philippians. Imagine being able to use the words *joy* and *rejoice* in a prison cell! In prison, Paul focused not on the decay and stench and powerlessness of his cell experience but on preaching the gospel. He writes, *"I rejoice. Yes, and I will continue to rejoice"* (Philippians 1:18 NIV).

Later in the book, he says, *"Rejoice in the Lord! It is no trouble for me to write the same things to you again, and it is a safeguard for you"* (Philippians 3:1 NIV), and *"Rejoice in the Lord always. I will say it again: Rejoice!"* (Philippians 4:4 NIV). Rejoicing in the Lord safeguards our spirit; it trains our hearts to focus on what is important in this aging season, as we move toward *"the prize for which God has called* [us] *heavenward in Christ Jesus"* (Philippians 3:14 NIV). Furthermore, rejoicing keeps us young at heart, turns the corners of our lips upward into a smile, and changes sour attitudes into joyful hope. We can always rejoice, no matter what our "cell" looks like.

My desire today is to *"rejoice in the Lord!"* As I start on my journey of promoting *Fabulous After 50*, and watch how God moves me to encourage others, I rejoice. God is already ahead of me. It is a divine appointment.

My goal today is to exalt Jesus as I age! Philippians chapter 2 says,

> *Wherefore God also hath highly exalted him, and given him a name which is above every name: that at the name of Jesus every knee should bow, of things in heaven, and things in earth, and things under the earth; and that every tongue should confess that Jesus Christ is Lord, to the glory of God the Father.*   (verses 9–11 KJV)

My prayer is that I would sow joy into the hearts of others. Lord, let me hear Your voice. I will sow Your Word, love, grace, and encouragement into others. My desire is *"that I may know Him, and the power of His resurrection and the fellowship of His sufferings, being conformed to His death"* (Philippians 3:10).

June 11, 2000

I have been weathered by the storms of life. I have gained strength from its winds. The crucible of life has given strength and resilience for my soaring spirit. I choose to soar through the decade of my 60s with majesty, strength, beauty, and freedom, like the eagle—king of the birds. Kenneth Price, in *The Eagle Christian*, wrote:

> Majesty is defined as the greatness and dignity of a sovereign and his grandeur. It is not a term that is used loosely with things of beauty, wealth, or strength, but is reserved only for those who possess all these things and more.
>
> The eagle, in flight, is all these things. His mastery of the awesome force of the wind, his beauty in flight, his strength in battle, his compassion for the young, and his all-encompassing eyesight are but a shadow of God.[7]

The strength of the eagle allows him to fly above the storms. His eyesight is eight times stronger than humans'. With his keen vision and infallible sense of direction, the magnificent bird sees storms approaching long before they arrive. Likewise, at age 62, I am equipped with a God-given spiritual insight, intuitiveness, and wisdom to see the storms of life approaching.

The eagle sits patiently, unafraid of the storm as it rumbles closer. When the winds begin to howl and the rain begins to fall, the eagle launches from his nest high on a cliff. He spreads his majestic wings, spanning six to ten feet, and flies into the face of the storm, using the strong gusts of wind to propel him. He circles round and round until he rises up over the storm and into the bright sunshine above the clouds.

As we age, the storms winds of life make us fly higher into the warm sunshine of God's love. While we might prefer the calmness, it is impossible to fly as high in the stillness as we can in the storm. I have learned that God's mercy is concealed within every storm cloud. His grace flows beneath every crosscurrent of wind. And faith in a living God gives us the freedom to soar sensationally after 60.

July 10, 2000

As I walked into the convention center, my heart pounded with anticipation. The festive atmosphere of New Orleans filled me, especially as I waited for my entry badge to get into the Christian Booksellers Association Convention. Throngs of people—from all around the nation and world—talked, laughed, listened, and strolled through the aisles of merchandise. I made my way through the crowd, looking for my publisher's booth.

As I rounded the corner to the booth, my eyes settled on dozens of copies of the original *Fabulous After 50* on display. I was overwhelmed. Tears filled my eyes as I prayed:

> Lord, I walk through the golden door of opportunity to glorify You as I encourage aging women to live better and longer. I ask You to speak through me so that Your wise words of power may influence people's lives.
>
> I also ask for poise under pressure. I ask for a keen memory. Turn on the lights in my brain to make new connections. Keep me healthy, humble, and happy to be doing Your work.
>
> Lord, You tell us in Your Word that we are Your ambassadors. Use me as Your ambassador. Amen.

August 3, 2000

> *He shall cover thee with his feathers, and under his wings shalt thou trust: his truth shall be thy shield and buckler.*
>
> (Psalm 91:4 KJV)

As a child on our tenant cotton farm, I remember a particular mother hen with about a dozen chicks, called "biddies," running freely in our backyard. When danger approached, the mother hen gathered every single fluffy chick under her big, outstretched wings. From wing tip to wing tip, the baby chicks snuggled under the mother's warm body. When danger came near, such as a threatening dog, she sat proudly and imperviously over her young chicks, and she did not move so that they wouldn't be visible. She stood strong against the enemy. Hovering under her protective body, those babies never knew any danger.

At 60-something, I trust in God just as those baby chicks trusted their mama hen. My future is secure in Him. At this stage, women are filled with many different emotions—hope, uncertainty, a sense of adventure, and expectancy, as well as fear. And, as we age, we become vulnerable in ways that we were not when we were "young chicks." But Scripture tell us that *"he that dwelleth in the secret place of the most High shall abide under the shadow of the Almighty"* (Psalm 91:1 KJV).

I love the image of God's shadow covering and protecting me, just as the hen covered her babies in my backyard so long ago. In this I can rest secure.

August 9, 2000

As I read the *Wall Street Journal* today, I found an article about 86-year-old Robert Mondavi, the patriarch of modern winemaking. In her article "The Property Report—Workplaces," author Nancy Hott wrote about Mr. Mondavi's commitment to his job. He still works every day and arrives at his office before 9 AM. But he reserves the right to nap on a soft leather couch with a pillow embroidered with the proverb, "Age does not matter unless you are wine."

As I continue to encourage women to age well, this proverb strikes a positive chord in me. It reminded me of my visit to Robert Mondavi Winery in Napa Valley, California, in 1998. After a tour, I read Mr. Mondavi's book, *Harvest of Joy: My Passion for Excellence*, and was reminded of Jesus' first miracle—turning water into wine.

Wine has always been a precious substance, especially in the first century, when it was difficult to keep water sterile. Yet Jesus' miracle still speaks to us today. John 2:1–12 (KJV) reads,

And the third day there was a marriage in Cana of Galilee; and the mother of Jesus was there: and both Jesus was called, and his disciples, to the marriage. And when they wanted wine, the mother of Jesus saith unto him, They have no wine. Jesus saith unto her, Woman, what have I to do with thee? mine hour is not yet come. His mother saith unto the servants, Whatsoever he saith unto you, do it. And there were set there six waterpots of stone, after the manner of the purifying of the Jews, containing two or three firkins apiece. Jesus saith unto them, Fill the waterpots with water. And they filled them up to the brim. And he saith unto them, Draw out now, and bear unto the governor of the feast. And they bare it. When the ruler of the feast had tasted the water that was made wine, and knew not whence it was: (but the servants which drew the water knew;) the governor of the feast called the bridegroom, and saith unto him, Every man at the beginning doth set forth good wine; and when men have well drunk, then that which is worse: but thou hast kept the good wine until now. This beginning of miracles did Jesus in Cana of Galilee, and manifested forth his glory; and his disciples believed on him. After this he went down to Capernaum, he, and his mother, and his brethren, and his disciples: and they continued there not many days.

Perhaps this is true of aging, as well. Jesus has kept the best for now! If wine gets better with age, so shall we!

August 9, 2000

As I stood at the hotel window, I thought about my 62nd birthday, which was only a few days away. I celebrated 38 of my birthdays with my husband. Now, as I fly solo after a painful divorce and start to feel again, I pray:

Thank You, Lord, for being a constant in my life. You never change. You never move. You never stop loving me.

Lord, as my 62nd birthday approaches, I feel that my life keeps changing like shifting sands. Yet I can count on You to steady me as I watch the glorious sunset each evening. I am a prisoner of hope, like Your Word says in Zechariah 9:12: *"Return to the stronghold, O prisoners who have the hope; this very day I am declaring that I will restore double to you."*

As I watched the sunset shine its glory
on the leaves below,
giving each leaf a special glow,
looking down at the tops of the trees,
two flags waving in the breeze,
God whispered to my heart,
"You are special to Me."

I prayed, tears falling on my chest,
"The birds are flying in couples, Lord.
The flags fly in couples, too.
God, I miss being a couple,
but You will come to my rescue."

What great beauty there is in Your earth,
creating such joy at the end of the day.
Your quietness fills my soul,
as the hush of night envelops my space.
  Amen.

September 16, 2000

Morning prayer: Thank You, Lord, for a new day! I am enamored of life! I feel balanced. It is one of those days when all systems are working in sync. I feel good. I am ready to get up and go!

Today, Scripture reminds me that my purpose is...

* to serve the Lord.

    Choose for yourselves today whom you will serve...as for me and my house, we will serve the LORD.
    (Joshua 24:15)

* to seek God's kingdom.

    But seek first His kingdom and His righteousness; and all these things shall be added to you.
    (Matthew 6:33)

* to do the Father's will.

    Jesus said to them, "My food is to do the will of Him who sent Me, and to accomplish His work....Lift up your eyes, and look on the fields, that they are white for harvest."
    (John 4:34–35)

* to finish the divine task.

    I glorified Thee on the earth, having accomplished the work which Thou hast given Me to do.
    (John 17:4)

- to complete the course.

> But I do not consider my life of any account as dear
> to myself, in order that I may finish my course, and
> the ministry which I received from the Lord Jesus, to
> testify solemnly of the gospel of the grace of God.
>
> (Acts 20:24)

September 22, 2000

Morning prayer: Lord, I have circled around the four seasons of the year 62 times. This life that You gave me is awesome. You have given me the ability to enjoy life, to be passionate about life, and to celebrate life. Thank You, Your Majesty! I will *"rejoice in the Lord always."*

Today I feel the WOW factor in my life. I do not think in terms of the number of years lived but in living each day to the fullest. Each day I reinvent myself. My focus is living, not aging. My plan is to be incessant—to keep moving and revving up my dreams. If I enjoy this life, what ecstasy heaven will be!

God said through Isaiah:

> Listen to me, all Israel who are left; I have created you
> and cared for you since you were born. I will be your God
> through all your lifetime, yes, even when your hair is white
> with age. I made you and I will care for you. I will carry you
> along and be your Savior.   (Isaiah 46:3–4 TLB)

Today, seniors are helping to write a golden chapter for aging Americans—and all the generations to follow. We are maintaining our youthful vigor and zeal for life. We are involved in the world around us. We are staying healthy by practicing good eating habits and by exercising. We keep raising the bar and exceeding expectations. We are striving for ageless living and endless energy. What a great time in history to be marching toward the age of 65. We can build our aging life on a faith that is eternal, on the God who never ages, and who lives outside the box of time.

———————————— • ● • ————————————

"Jesus is turning my life and my family from water into wine—the beginning of miracles."
—Shirley W. Mitchell's Diary

———————————— • ● • ————————————

QUESTIONS FOR REFLECTION AND APPLICATION

1. If you meditate and journal, what new goals can you set to improve this time of devotion with God?

2. If you do not meditate and journal, what is keeping you from doing so? How might these practices benefit you?

3. After meditating and journaling, ask yourself what kind of deeper thoughts this time has spurred.

SEVEN SECRETS OF MEDITATING AND JOURNALING

1. Meditating on God's promises will help you to live a balanced life.

2. Journaling helps because it gets your thoughts onto paper so that you can work with them.

3. Meditating on God's Word reassures us that God is in control.

4. Meditating and journaling help to relieve pent-up frustration and stress.

5. These practices are quiet oases in a busy world.

6. They help you to understand yourself better.

7. They also help you to experience intimacy with God.

LONGEVITY PROMISE

*"Trust in the LORD with all your heart and lean not on
your own understanding; in all your ways acknowledge
him, and he will make your paths straight."*
—Proverbs 3:5–6 (NIV)

Endnotes

1. *USA Today* (January 2000).

2. Dotson Rader, "I Knew God Would Never Let Me Down,"
   Parade magazine (17 December 2000): 4–6.

3. Bob Moore, *You Can Be President (Or Anything Else)* (Gretna,
   LA: Pelican Publishing Company, 1980), 128.

4. John Schaar, as quoted by Robert M. McChesney in his
   President's Message, *Montevallo Today* XC, no. 1 (Winter
   2000): 3.

5. Wayne Muller, "The Real Jubilee," *Forbes* magazine (27
   December 1999): 310.

6. Corrie ten Boom, *The Hiding Place* (Carmel NY: Guideposts,
   Associates, Inc., 1971), preface.

7. Kenneth Price, *The Eagle Christian* (Wetumpka, AL: Old
   Faithful Press, 1984), 56.

CHAPTER 6

SENSATIONAL GRANDPARENTING

"To have grandchildren is not only to be given something but to be given something back.....It is mainly because of [your grandchildren] that the earth will not be as if you never walked on it."[1]
—Frederick Buechner

"Grandchildren are the crown of old men, and the glory of sons is their fathers."
—Proverbs 17:6

The screen door slapped shut behind me as I raced outside. I crossed the lawn and ran into Mamma Todd's home. Delicious smells wafted through my grandmother's kitchen window and into our house—I knew she'd just filled the 25-pound flour bag with fresh tea cakes. She always hung the bag from a small hook on the wall at just the right height for little hands to reach.

Mamma Todd would be making millions if she were a chef today. Indelible memories are etched in my heart: a large table filled with dishes made from fresh-picked vegetables from the garden; being surrounded by my big family—uncles, aunts, cousins, and grandparents. Sunday dinner brought all the relatives together, including the preacher and his family, as well as anyone else who might need a plate of scrumptious food and a big helping of love and acceptance.

Shirley's family in the cotton field. Mamma Todd is at the far left,
Paw Paw is just to the right of the telephone pole,
and brother Buck is at the far right on top of the wagon.
Fifteen-year-old Shirley is in the middle of the picture,
with her arm resting on the truck.

There were times when 50 people showed up for our holiday meal. Paw Paw would preside over the table, seated at the head, and always prayed a long prayer before we ate. We grandchildren squinted through our eyelids, jostled ankles under the table, and tried not to snicker while we waited impatiently for the "Amen." Sixty years later, I can still hear the chatter of the happy people who ate and enjoyed fellowship around the table.

Grandparents impart many gifts to their grandchildren, including love and acceptance. What a privilege it is to pass this love on to my own seven grandchildren and to replicate the joyful, rambunctious mealtimes I shared with my own grandparents years before.

GREAT GRANDPARENTING

My daughter, Karen, is raising three of my granddaughters in Cincinnati—Michelle, Monica, and Melissa. I'm thrilled when my "Three Ms" visit me. It calls for a house party, and my son David's three children, Stephanie, Sarah, and Jackson, join in the fun. Lawrence, the son of my youngest child, Jay, is the youngest of the grandchildren. Lawrence is always the subject of "oohs" and "aahs" when everyone gets together. Over the weekend, we have a big, noisy party, filled with many activities, such as jumping on the bed, watching movies while eating popcorn, and refusing to sleep for Grandmother. I have a room for the grandchildren that is complete with games, a pool table, a big television set, and cold soda pop. This room is always filled with laughter.

When my grandchildren are on summer break, the party may last for a week. Friends pop in and out, adding to the excitement—and the general din! We watch home movies; play Twister, pool, and dodgeball; and sing karaoke—our favorite. The grandchildren get very creative with song and dance, working up routines and practicing for days before performing for their parents after Sunday lunch.

There is nothing like being a part of a child's life again, and grandparenting is a perfect way to add energy and spice to our own lives, as well as to the lives of our grandchildren.

GIFTS FROM GRANDPARENTS TO GRANDCHILDREN

God had a great plan in store when He created grandparents: He gave them laps for holding, arms for hugging, cheeks for snuggling, and hearts for believing the best about their grandchildren.

Whether you are a traditional grandmother—nurturing flowers in the garden and baking cookies in the oven—or active in career or travel, or both, you are in the perfect season in your 60s for making a difference in young lives. What a privilege it is be considered part of a child's growth and development.

My granddaughter Monica made this clear to me when she was four years old. "What is your name?" she asked me.

"Shirley is my name," I replied.

"No, Shirley is not your name!" shouted Monica. "Your name is Grandmother!"

The majority of people over the age of 65 are grandparents. There are millions of grandparents! Think of the wisdom, life experience, goodness, and laughter they possess and can share with younger generations. We can make a difference in a generation that has been raised in day care and has seen more divorce than any other generation to date—a generation in which the majority of mothers are employed at least part-time.

My mother told me that when my grandmother Hattie came to visit us, she would walk in the fields behind our home, kneel down in the dirt, and pray loudly for me by name. Today I can still feel the effect of those prayers and the love she had for me. Whether we are biological grandmothers or not, whether our grandchildren live close by or far away, we can still powerfully, positively, and prayerfully impact the lives of the younger generation.

The Gift of One-on-One Time

A terrific way to invest in our grandchildren is to arrange solo visits. Whether your one-on-one time with your grandchildren is a weekend at home, an off-site field trip, a camping trip, or a tea outing, this time will build them up for life. To make sure that I spent this much-needed one-on-one time with my grandchildren, I decided, when my oldest granddaughter, Michelle, turned ten, that I would take each grandchild on a weeklong trip of his or her choice when he or she turned ten.

Michelle chose to go to Washington, D.C. Her first request on the trip was to travel by stretch limo from the airport to the hotel. What a ride! At the hotel, the limousine driver allowed Michelle to stand with her head out of the sunroof for me to take a picture. During our week together, we toured the Capitol and many museums, and we enjoyed a different restaurant for dinner each night. The one-on-one interaction we shared while enjoying new sights, activities, food, fun, and frolic created a stronger bond and formed wonderful memories for us both.

Shirley with her grandchildren

Though she was only ten, Michelle looked 15 years of age. When we boarded a trolley to tour Washington, the driver would not sell Michelle a child's ticket. That pleased her, because she, of course, wanted to look older. As I followed Michelle onto the trolley, I held out my money to the driver and said, "Senior citizen." Because the driver did not believe I was a senior citizen, I had to pay full price, but I didn't mind! Michelle wanted to be older, while I loved being considered younger!

Monica, Michelle's sister, couldn't wait for her grandmother/granddaughter adventure. She, too, chose our nation's capital. Because she was a swimmer, the highlight of the trip for her was swimming in the Olympic-sized swimming pool at the hotel. We ate breakfast daily in the hotel café, where Monica's outgoing personality won the hearts of the servers. They were very gracious and gave her extra desserts.

For her tenth birthday, my granddaughter Stephanie chose a week with Grandmother in New York City. Our room overlooked Times Square. Excitement, glitter, lights, and the sounds of the city were so tangible. Stephanie photographed the skyline as we circled Ellis Island and saw the Statue of Liberty. We even got to see the World Trade Center before 9/11. Of the adventures in New York City, she most enjoyed seeing the Broadway show *The Lion King*.

Spending the week with this beautiful child filled my emotional tank to the brim, as did the following year's trip to Hollywood with Melissa. Lovely Melissa, from Cincinnati, and charming Sarah, from Alabama, experienced Los Angeles together. As they entered the suite in the Renaissance Hollywood Hotel, they jumped, giggled, skipped, and squealed, "I love this room!" The window offered an excellent view of the famous Hollywood sign, perched high on Mount Lee—the tallest peak in L.A.

These girls gleamed as they stood in the footprints of their favorite stars on outside Grauman's Chinese Theatre. We spent hours at the Universal Studios theme park. They giggled their way through a caricature by a local artist, and the resulting piece of art now enjoys a place of pride in my home.

The restaurant at our hotel served a rich chocolate cake, and every night before we retired to the room, the girls finished off their full day with the sweet treat. The only thing Melissa and Sarah did not accomplish that week was writing a book about their adventures in Hollywood. Oh, well—maybe someday.

In the future, my two grandsons, Jackson and Lawrence, will accompany me on a trip of their choice when they reach 10 years of age. I look forward to this precious time.

The Gift of Faith

While we receive many gifts from our grandchildren and, in turn, impart gifts to them, perhaps no gift is as important as the legacy we share with them when we pass on our faith. In the Bible, Timothy credited his faith to his grandmother. Paul wrote to Timothy, saying, *"I have been reminded of your sincere faith, which first lived in your grandmother Lois…and, I am persuaded, now lives in you also"* (2 Timothy 1:5 NIV). The name Lois has gone down in history, changing the very course of the world—not because she was rich and famous, but because she believed in the Lord Jesus and shared Him with her children and grandchildren.

My friend Marta invites her grandchildren to stay with her as often as possible, and she finds great joy in tucking them into bed at night. She kneels beside her own bed every night and prays for them out loud. She prays regularly that they will come to salvation, find Christian friends, and experience continued spiritual growth in the future.

Louise's grandchildren jump with joy at her visits. They clamor about her, eager to tell stories, and just as eager to hear hers. "Did you bring the people?" they ask. Louise smiles, reaches for her bag, and pulls out little carved wooden people, along with a few props. In her gentle voice, she begins to tell a story. Jesus, Daniel, Ruth, or some other key figure in Scripture comes to life as she moves the wooden people about. The children sit and watch, breathless.

Next, it is their turn to tell the story. And Louise's faith, which was learned at her own grandmother's knee when she came to America from Germany, is passed down to yet another generation.

Grandparents Put the "Quality" in "Quality Time"

The following is a short list of activities to help you to connect with your grandchildren, as well as to enhance the time that you spend together.

- Teach grandchildren to cook your family's traditional dishes.
- Take a leisurely vacation together.
- Tell them stories of your childhood.
- Play games together, from board games to card games to outdoor games.
- Host a family dinner after a christening or the baptism of a child.
- Invite them to help you decorate your home for the holidays.
- Give special gifts to your grandchildren, such as toys, books, a Bible, or a special stuffed animal.
- Record yourself reading a book aloud and send it to your grandchildren to listen to.

- Show them faith in action by serving others.

- Visit nursing homes together.

- Write letters to them regularly.

- Send them encouraging e-mails and/or letters.

- Share with them tidbits of wisdom you have learned.

- Ask questions about their day, their thoughts, and their interests, and listen to them.

- Hold them. Hug them. Laugh with them. They will never forget the attention that you give them!

GIFTS FROM GRANDCHILDREN TO GRANDPARENTS

The beauty of relationships between grandchildren and grandparents is that, though we have a lot of gifts to give our grandchildren, we are the ones who benefit the most from the relationship. Now we will consider the gifts that grandchildren give to their grandparents.

The Gift of Meaning

Hard times had hardened Naomi's heart. Her husband died after moving her to a foreign land, and when famine struck, her two sons died, as well, leaving her with two daughters-in-law and no grandchildren to carry on her husband's lineage. In her despair and grief, she set out to return to her homeland, Bethlehem, in Judah.

In a display of rare loyalty, Naomi's daughter-in-law Ruth decided to travel with her. When they arrived, Naomi's despair turned into determination, and she and Ruth developed a plan to live on the land. Ruth would glean in the fields of a male relative, a rich and eligible bachelor, and make herself invaluable to him.

Their plan worked. Amid much blessing form the townspeople, Boaz married Ruth. But, when Ruth left home, Naomi was alone again, with no purpose except to wait for grandchildren.

So Boaz took Ruth, and she became his wife, and he went in to her. And the Lord enabled her to conceive, and she gave birth to a son. Then the women said to Naomi, "Blessed is the LORD *who has not left you without a redeemer today, and may his name become famous in Israel. May he also be to you a restorer of life and a sustainer of your old age; for your daughter-in-law, who loves you and is better to you than seven sons, has given birth to him." Then Naomi took the child and laid him in her lap, and became his nurse. And the neighbor women gave him a name, saying, "A son has been born to Naomi!" So they named him Obed. He is the father of Jesse, the father of David.* (Ruth 4:13–17)

Remember who David's "great-great-grandson" was? Jesus. Naomi was blessed and was given a heritage from God—a grandson to carry on the family name. Naomi's response to Obed brought life to many—including her own withered heart. Grandchildren are a heritage from God.

The Gift of Surprise

Many seniors say that when they first became grandparents, they were not prepared for the emotions that accompanied their new role. Fortunately, the surprise abates. Martha Bolton, author of *Cooking with Hot Flashes*, told me this story:

Something was up. My husband made me cancel an appointment during my birthday week but wouldn't be specific as to when I could reschedule. He would only say, "Keep the first week of September open." The night before my birthday, I was at my computer when the doorbell rang. My husband asked me to get it, as he was busy.

All I could see in the dark was a large gift box sitting at the foot of my front porch steps. I looked back at my husband, who had followed me to the door. He smiled sheepishly.

"Go open it."

Seeing the size of the box, I asked, "Do I open it outside or bring it in?"

"Open it out there," he said.

My mind went to what might be awaiting me in the box. A dog? Cat? Llama? Plant? Approaching the box, I could see that it wasn't completely closed, so I went back to the animal list. Only ribbon loosely connected the flaps. Cautiously, I went to open the flaps, and out popped something. Several "somethings," as a matter of fact.

It was my grandchildren, Kiana and Kadin, from California. Then, my son and his wife jumped out from behind the bushes. My two other sons and my other daughter-in-law, as well as my husband, had all been in on the surprise. What a wonderful present!

Whether they jump out of a box or call us on the phone, grandchildren are constantly surprising us with the gift of adventure and excitement.

The Gift of Self-esteem

God sent grandchildren because He knew that in middle age, we would need true love and attention. Nothing compares with the joy of being loved by a beaming child who calls you "Grandmother." I once met a child on a plane who was en route to visit her grandmother, and she wrote me this poem:

"OLD"

The body of my grandmother looks old,
    yet she is young in her soul.
Her walk is a slow pace,
    yet she could win the human race.
Some people think she's no fun,
    yet I think she's #1!

Being around our grandchildren can tighten our sagging self-esteem. The world judges us for our wrinkles and extra pounds, but grandkids love us with no reservations.

When my granddaughter Monica called from Cincinnati to invite me to visit her school, I jumped on a plane. Her school project entailed choosing a book and giving a report as though she were the author.

Monica selected my book *Fabulous After 50*. With poise and confidence, she presented her report. I stood in the hallway, just outside the room, and peeked through the door at my beautiful granddaughter speaking in front of the class. Tears filled my eyes as I watched her, dressed as I would dress, speaking in my Southern accent, and mimicking my hand gestures. (I never realized she observed me so closely.) After her report, she announced to her classmates with excitement, "And now, I would like to introduce you to the real Shirley Mitchell."

I hope I live to be 120 years old, like Moses did! Otherwise, there just won't be enough time to fully enjoy my grandchildren. Isn't longevity a gift to grandparents? I read an article in *Time* magazine titled "How to Live to Be 100," which stated that "playing with...grandkids can lengthen your life."[2] That sounds good to me! I have plans for every single one of those days.

SO, YOU AREN'T A GRANDMOTHER?
ADOPT A GRANDCHILD!

Let's face it. Kids are life-giving, especially when they are a generation removed, and the great responsibility of raising a child belongs to our children! But perhaps this life-giving opportunity has not come to you yet, or maybe your grandchildren live far away. There is still a vital ministry waiting for you, down the street, or maybe even right next door! With years of life and love and experience and wisdom under your belt, you can pour into the lives of children who do not have grandparents of their own.

When a couple in church asked Judy if she could babysit their newborn son twice a week, Judy and her husband knew that their lives would change. Her part-time job would get shoved into other nooks during the week, she would be tired, and her time would be eaten up. But when she held the baby in her arms, she just knew that it was the right thing to do. She and Tom would "adopt" this baby as their own grandchild, giving him their heart, their time, and their years' worth of wisdom and experience—an opportunity they did not have with their own children. Since then, another baby has joined them on their "grandparent" days. And the joy of telling the children about Jesus, of offering them endless play and patience, has changed the lives of both families.

Perhaps your grandchildren live too far away—too far to feel your loving arms about them, too far to see you sitting on the bleachers at their games or in the audience at their performances. Love them long-distance and, as you do, fill the holes in your heart by loving some children nearby. In our transient society, millions of children must let themselves into their own homes after school; they have no significant contact with older adults, and they are consequently ripe for trouble—or nurture.

In reference to grandparents who are making a difference in children's lives, Roger Palms wrote,

> Praise God that many are saying yes to the opportunities around them to be grandmas and grandpas. They don't act old, just mature. They recognize that the over-65 population…is a wonderful army for good. That means no child should be without a grandparent on his street or in his church or at the teen drop-in center. No young parent should be without an older encourager or helper nearby.[3]

With 11 million single-parent homes in America, think of the possibilities. Every family represents heartbreak—and a world of ministry potential! Susan Graham Mathis, editorial director of Focus on the Family, said,

> Single-parent families are called "the hidden mission field," and for good reason. Often they have little or no connection to other church families, and their immediate or extended family may live far away. We can use our gifts, time, or resources to help them. Some of us are gifted in prayer, mentoring, teaching, financial counseling, child-care, or organizing special events—all things that can help single parents…. Being a grandparent to a single-parent child is one of the best ways to aid these families.[4]

We don't have to go on a short-term mission trips across the continent or other countries to make a difference. Eleven million families are holding up their arms and saying, "Pick me! Adopt me!" Yes, it might be messy. Anytime other people enter the picture, paint is spilled. But giving meaning to others' lives is why we are still breathing. Imagine—we can choose to be a blessing, all over again.

WHEN GRANDMOTHERS BECOME MOMS—AGAIN

When Alice's daughter died of cancer, Alice took over the role of mother. At age 81, she makes sure the kids have clean clothes for school, presses her cheek against their foreheads to check for fevers, schedules physicals, and meets with their teachers. And she prays over the children regularly, holding them close, both physically and spiritually, and asks God to help the family grieve over their enormous loss and find life again.

She is tired. Her heart aches. Her stress levels are elevated. She has revised her hopes and dreams for the latter half of her life. Though her finances are stretched taut, her new responsibility fills her life with meaning, with a reason to get up in the morning.

Alice is not alone. According to the U.S. Census Bureau, in 2010, there were 7 million grandparents caring for grandchildren younger than 18.[5] That is a lot of children! That means that instead of putting up their feet or packing their luggage for an exciting trip, these grandparents have become aged parents. They have exchanged retirement for homework, sporting events, and trips to the school. Many of them must rejoin the workforce in order to make ends meet.

Churches, hospitals, and support groups are coming alongside these valiant grandparents by offering counseling, companionship, and a place to explore the pains and possibilities of a second round of parenting. Message boards and online groups offer a place to exchange ideas and vent, a spot to give and receive encouragement for a hard new reality.[6]

"We might have chosen a different set of circumstances for our child and grandchildren, but we are glad we are able to care for our grandkids in this way," these second-time parents seem to say.

If you are in this situation, please do not try to do it alone. Find people to support and encourage you, to relieve you of your responsibility for a night, and to swap ideas. Also know that God is dancing with joy over you as you care for the precious children He has entrusted to you.

WHEN GRANDCHILDREN DISAPPOINT

Sometimes, though, this grandparenting thing isn't all it's cracked up to be. Images of shining-faced children and straight-A report cards do not reflect every grandmother's reality.

Rebecah wept over her son's late-night phone call with the news that her grandchild had been hospitalized for a drug addiction. She prayed for the family and stayed supportive. She called regularly to offer a listening ear, always asking, "What can I do to help?" Her grandchild never felt judged by her.

What about the pain of having under-functioning grandchildren? It helps to keep in touch with our feelings—to acknowledge our disappointment and to honor it instead of pushing it aside. We need to work through the pain by supporting the family, staying in touch, and praying. It helps to find who can share the journey with you. Too many grandparents feel that they must be silent if their kids or grandkids haven't turned out perfectly. But grandparenting provides a perfect opportunity to *"rejoice with those who rejoice, and weep with those who weep"* (Romans 12:15).

Perhaps the disappointment lies in broken relationships—our children or grandchildren have hurt us, ignored us, or been angry with us. As the family matriarchs, we must not sit around moping because they won't call or visit. Life has taught us to do better than that! Instead, we are to reach out, model forgiveness, and seek to mend fences and reestablish relationships.

The Missing Generation

Perhaps you have known the heartbreak of having a child abort a baby—your grandchild. In 2008, there were 1.8 million abortions.[7] The largest number of these abortions were performed on women 25 years of age or younger. Abortions affect a lot more than just the mother. They also affect the lives of the would-be parents and grandparents. This is a grief and a loss that grandparents do not often voice. But the silence doesn't diminish their pain.

Jayne Schooler, author of *Mom, Dad, I'm Pregnant: When Your Daughter or Son Faces an Unplanned Pregnancy*, said,

> It is a place where a Christian mother never expects to be—living with the reality that her daughter and/or son chose an abortion for her grandchild. For these mothers, the losses are innumerable, the pain overwhelming, silent, suffering, suffocating. There is rarely someone with whom to share this most devastating circumstance.
>
> When a Christian mother learns of her daughter's abortion, guilt floods her—what did she do to cause this? Grief and loss shadow her as she ponders the realities of what might have been. Shame becomes a constant companion because of the forced secrecy she feels demanded of her.

The message for these mothers is twofold: first, don't keep silent but reach out to a trusted friend. Second, believe and know that God is a God of restoration. His desire, more than anything else, is for the restoration of your relationship with your daughter, as well as for her life to reflect His forgiving grace.

THE GIFT OF TECHNOLOGY:
LONG-DISTANCE GRANDPARENTING

Do you remember when a "web" was a spider's home? You are definitely part of the older generation if the first thing that comes to mind when you hear the word "mouse" is a rodent. If you would have told me 20 years ago that I would be writing this book with a hand on a mouse, I would have thought you were from the planet Mars.

When I was a child, a "ram" referred to a male sheep; a "byte" left teeth prints. "Memory" was what grandmothers had lost. Sending letters the traditional way is now called "snail mail," in contrast to the instant communication of e-mail. My granddaughters from Cincinnati would rather chat via e-mail than send a letter.

Aging is constant change, like shifting shadows. The shades of change can be exciting, magical, and fruitful when we focus on the positives. Age may become a dance of mounting intrigue and new horizons. One new horizon of intrigue is learning how to use the computer or the iPad for faster communication with our grandchildren. This is especially true for grandmothers who have long-distance relationships with their grandchildren.

It seems that grandchildren handle the computer with great ease, while grandmothers struggle with the intricacies of this modern machine. Charlene's grandkids gave her a computer for Christmas and set up an e-mail account for her so that they can communicate with her while at college. Now a widow, Charlene finds new life in writing to her grandchildren and hearing from them, far more often than in her B.C. (before computer) days.

Learning how to use to the computer is not only a challenging adventure; it makes our grandchildren accessible 24/7 (to borrow one of their phrases). Computers enhance our grandparenting and provide a place for our grandchildren to share and receive love, attention, and time. (They also make us look cool in our grandkids' eyes, which is no small benefit!) With so many negative messages popping into their inboxes daily, what fun it must be for them to see an e-mail from their grandmother—a message that communicates, loving them, reminding them of values and faith and character, and calling them forward to be who they were created to be.

Jesus said in John 10:10, "*My purpose is to give life in all its fullness*" (NLT). When grandkids enter the picture, our lives feel full. And with our lives full, we are in a perfect position to pour into the lives of the young generation. We can make the most of our age, experience, and life lessons by passing them on to our children.

In so doing, the story comes around again, and we realize Jesus spoke the truth when He said, "*Unless you are converted and become like children, you shall not enter the kingdom of heaven. Whoever then humbles himself as this child, he is the greatest in the kingdom of heaven*" (Matthew 18:3–4). Grandchildren move us closer to heaven.

—————————— • ● • ——————————

"As we watch our grandchildren grow, we realize we will live on after our death."
—Shirley W. Mitchell's Diary

—————————— • ● • ——————————

QUESTIONS FOR REFLECTION AND APPLICATION

1. Your grandchildren are, in a sense, your perpetual youth. If you have grandchildren, how would you rate your relationship with them? How do you plan to connect with each one and stay in touch?

2. What possibilities are there for starting or joining a group of grandmothers where you can share ideas, carry each other's hardships, and search Scripture for spiritual guidance? Consider options in your neighborhood, at church, or in a community center.

3. If you don't have grandchildren, think about the children who live near you in your community or who attend your church. What do you know about their families? How might you invest in their lives?

4. If you are currently the primary caregiver for a grandchild, what concerns do you have? Who walks along that journey with you? What support do you have? What are the frustrations? The joys?

SEVEN GIFTS THAT GRANDPARENTS GIVE TO GRANDCHILDREN

1. Cheerful smiles
2. Faith
3. History
4. Hugs
5. Laps to sit on
6. Laughter
7. Unconditional love and acceptance

SEVEN GIFTS THAT GRANDCHILDREN GIVE TO GRANDPARENTS

1. Hope
2. Laughter

3. A legacy

4. Meaning

5. Memories

6. Touch

7. Unconditional love

LONGEVITY PROMISE

"Blessed are all who fear the LORD, *who walk in his ways....May the* LORD *bless you from Zion all the days of your life; may you see the prosperity of Jerusalem, and may you live to see your children's children."*
—Psalm 128:1, 5–6 (NIV)

Endnotes

1. Frederick Buechner, *Beyond Words* (San Francisco, CA: HarperCollins, 2004), 139–140.

2. Richard Corliss and Michael D. Lemonick, "How to Live to Be 100," *Time* magazine (30 August 2004): 40.

3. Palms, *Celebrate Life After 50*, 126.

4. Susan Graham Mathis, "Good Samaritans for Single Parents," *Focus on the Family* magazine (April 2004): 21.

5. See www.census.gov for more statistics.

6. See www.aarp.com for a grandparents' support group listing.

7. Rachel Jones and Kathryn Kooistra, "Abortion Incidence and Access to Services in the United States," *Perspectives on Sexual and Reproductive Health* 43, no. 1 (2011): 41–50.

CHAPTER 7

COPING WITH LOSS IN MIDLIFE

*"One of the problems is our narrowed definition of grief:
mourning the death of another….grief involves far more
than physical loss of life. Grief is about other losses, as well:
dreams, bodily function, roles, relationships, and unfulfilled
expectations of those relationships."[1]*
—Jane Rubietta, *Quiet Places*

*"Truly, truly, I say to you, unless a grain of wheat
falls into the earth and dies, it remains by itself alone;
but if it dies, it bears much fruit."*
—John 12:24

My spirits soared as I walked down the long, winding driveway to the mailbox near the road. I could not stop smiling at the brilliance of the bright fall sunshine. The cool breeze gave me zest as I opened the box lid. I struggled to pull the large, brown business envelope out of the box. When I saw that the return addressee was my husband's lawyer, my heart skipped a beat.

Fortunately, I waited to open the envelope until I had returned to the house and was sitting on the sofa. With shaking hands, I slit it open, and I immediately recognized the divorce papers. The finality of the struggle we had been experiencing hit me full force, with blurred vision, heart palpitations, and hot flashes. I almost fainted. This moment marked the beginning of a long, painful struggle that would profoundly affect my life and the lives of my family members.

WAVES OF CHANGE

My husband, Jack, and I spent hours lounging on the beach, enjoying the hot sun, the melodic ocean sounds, and the gleeful chatter of the people on the shoreline. We laughed and splashed in the water and built a magnificent sand castle. Walking away from the huge creation at sunset, I knew that the gorgeous sand structure would be washed away by the tide during the night.

Years later, I think about how the beautiful structure of our 38-year marriage was washed away by the tides of middle-age discontent, business and family pressures, and unresolved differences.

I was so busy raising my children and helping build the family business that I pushed aside the undercurrents that threatened our marriage. A photo of my husband and me at a formal dinner showed the truth: there was a handsome couple seated together at a banquet table, with 12 inches separating them. Our bodies were turned half away from each other. Only our heads were together, facing the camera.

When Jack filed for divorce, I felt as though the ocean had swept me up and tugged me out to sea, pulling along with me everything we had so carefully built—a family, a home, and a business. And, like many others, I had to learn how to cope with loss in midlife.

THE EFFECTS OF MIDLIFE LOSS

Many types of loss sweep through our lives, especially in our middle years. In our 60s, we often face more changes than in any other season of life.

For Jeannette, the waves of change began to crash upon her at the news that her husband had been diagnosed with both Parkinson's and Alzheimer's diseases. Her own mental state and physical health are sound, her husband's memory and physical abilities are weakened more and more each day. Along with losing the man she married, Jeannette must revise her dreams to travel, volunteer, and continue life's adventure side by side with her husband. Her life is now centered on caring for him.

In her 60s, Diane was forced to leave her job of 15 years, and to forfeit its benefits, when she moved to Iowa. Even with 35 years of impeccable work experience, she struggled to find suitable employment. Diane finally found a job in a field similar to that of her field of expertise, and she worked double the hours of the other employees in order to learn the new coding, language, and etiquette of the job. Then, one day, before all of her retirement benefits had kicked in, the office manager fired her. As if dealing with a new home, a new town, and a new job were not enough, losing her job totally wrecked her self-esteem. So far, Diane has not been able to find another full-time position, and she has signed on with a temporary agency—without benefits—to make ends meet.

Donna's husband was working on the roof one day when he fell off and died. What an unexpected, tragic loss.

Kathy enjoyed vibrant health until a routine visit to her doctor revealed that she had a tumor behind her eyes. Her battle to live well with cancer and pay the health-care bills created a new, unexpected agenda for her sixth decade of life.

The pain of grieving over loss in all its forms is compounded by blame, low self-esteem, loneliness, and loss of identity, which trickle in, unnoticed, until we are up to our necks in water.

Blame

Susan blamed her ex-husband for landing her in loss in midlife. Laura blamed herself for her husband's affair, which fissured their relationship. As Colleen cared for her aging parents, she blamed them for not making better provisions for themselves for old age.

The problem of blame is that it does not solve anything; it only deepens the quicksand of loss. We must hold ourselves accountable for where will we go from here. How we got to the place of loss is less important than how we will move through it.

Low Self-worth

Living in a world that reveres youth can wreak havoc on our sense of self-worth. Losses of such things as health and ability, as well as changes in our relationships or jobs, can lower our self-esteem. When retirees no longer receive affirmation of their value on a consistent basis through paychecks, they may ask themselves, "What am I worth?"

You are worth more than the world, and you are the reason God created the heavens and the earth in the first place! Ask God to show you His love and to care for you, especially in these very real losses.

Loneliness

Perhaps one of the greatest impacts of loss is loneliness. Living solo in a "couples' world" leaves many women feeling undesirable and unattractive. These feelings are compounded when they blame themselves for their loss, or when their self-esteem takes a nosedive like a balloon tied to a brick.

Furthermore, loss and grief can be very isolating, even when we share our experiences with a spouse or a dear friend. The more we isolate ourselves, the more we cut ourselves off from the vital avenue of healing that God provides. God has told us from the very beginning, *"It is not good for the man to be alone"* (Genesis 2:18).

Loss of Identity

"Who am I?" is a question that recurs throughout life, particularly when loss washes over us, in one form or another, and causes us to lose our bearings. It is normal to ask this question when we retire, move, find ourselves suddenly solo, or face declining health or compromised physical ability. The sooner we figure out that our worth is unrelated to our looks or accomplishments, the sooner we can accept our bodies and move on with our lives.

Depression

Geri plummeted into depression when her husband lost both his job and his health. Her heart was so heavy that she would rarely get out of bed. When familiar and beloved parts of our world change, often against our will, it is important to notice what happens in our spirit. Recognizing symptoms of depression is a vital first step in moving toward healing. Please do not choose to "just live" with the feeling. Seek a counselor or a wise friend to help shine light in the darkness. There is no shame in the issue, but, as we pay attention, we can begin to find hope.

STRUGGLING IN GOD'S LOVING ARMS

During my 38 years of marriage, I had built a lovely life—a family, with a home, engaged in the local community, and involved in a church. I loved my rich, full, joyful days and the vibrant family life that evolved around me. At the age of 60, I dreamed of a future that involved slowing down, spending quality time with my husband, and traveling.

At this time, my two older children were happily married and professionally successful, and my youngest child was still in college. With less responsibility and more free time, I was just beginning to enjoy the empty nest when my husband asked for a divorce. After the divorce was official, my house became a large, quiet, empty tomb. My life, as I had known it, disappeared.

For the first time, I understood the meaning of a broken heart. The intense pain of loss literally hurt my heart. Tears flowed freely. Raw emotions brought tears to my eyes when I least expected them. At this point, I could have become an emotional cripple.

But I felt God's loving arms holding me. He allowed me to feel the pain, but He also provided His strength. The security of God's presence around me in the midst of pain and fear was indescribable. After filling me with Scripture for years, God brought Isaiah 53:4–7 to my mind:

Surely our griefs He Himself bore, and our sorrows He carried; yet we ourselves esteemed Him stricken, smitten of God, and afflicted. But He was pierced through for our transgressions, He was crushed for our iniquities; the chastening for our well-being fell upon Him, and by His scourging we are healed. All of us like sheep have gone astray, each of us has turned to his own way; but the LORD has caused the iniquity of us all to fall on Him. He was oppressed and He was afflicted, yet He did not open His mouth; like a lamb that is led to slaughter, and like a sheep that is silent before its shearers, so He did not open His mouth.

This trial did not wreck me. My Savior knew my pain, and He had taken my bruises upon Himself. Healing would come. The Word of God, hidden in my heart, gave me stability in this storm of life.

As I stood in the doorway of change and choice, God whispered to my heart, "While making the shift to solo living, don't just survive. *Prevail*."

As we steer through the rocks and weeds of midlife loss, we may feel despair and fear; we may fall facedown in the sand. However, we can—and we must—pick ourselves up. We must stand up, look up, have a positive attitude, and keep going forward.

We will prevail, because God will not fail.

PREVAILING STRATEGIES

Quiet Time with the Lord

As I struggled in God's loving arms through the divorce, I wrote these words in my journal:

Shirley, make the best thing in your life out of your worst experience. Being separated from my husband is like being in solitary confinement. People who usually talked to me or called me on the phone are now quiet. They do not know what to say. My children support me but are confused. This situation is new for all of us. Faith, self-confidence, a new career, and improving my life and surroundings: these have been my salvation.

I must walk through new doors into new adventures. Only as I walk through adversity hand in hand with

God will the waters of adversity part before me and open upon new life.

Prevailing doesn't have to be complicated; sometimes, it just means doing the right thing. We prevail when we build our lives on the Rock, pay attention to the longing of our heart, and choose to nourish the needs of our soul.

In a place of devastation, Elijah begged God for help, and the Lord said to him:

> *"Go out and stand on the mountain in the presence of the* Lord, *for the* Lord *is about to pass by." Then a great and powerful wind tore the mountains apart and shattered the rocks before the* Lord, *but the* Lord *was not in the wind. After the wind there was an earthquake, but the* Lord *was not in the earthquake. After the earthquake came a fire, but the* Lord *was not in the fire. And after the fire came a gentle whisper.*   (1 Kings 19:11–12 NIV)

Women in their 60s are veterans of personal grief, to some degree. Each night, just before sleep puts its blanket of peace over me, I felt a few moments of deep loss in the days and months following my divorce. And those were the times when I heard the still, small voice of God and felt His presence.

I rekindle my faith each day with quiet time with the Lord. God's Word speaks to my heart. I speak to Him through prayer; I sit and listen to Him; and He renews me, day after day.

When loss makes you feel like you are lying on your back in a deep, dark pit, it's time to listen for the still, small voice of God and to remember that there's no place to go but up. The path out of pain is to feel the pain of loss and then to deal with that loss. Walking that path with prayer, family, friends, support groups, meaningful activities, and regular church attendance will keep us from the pitfalls of grief and resentment.

Films to Refocus

As I struggled to maintain my sanity following my divorce, I deliberately participated in activities that would empower me, edify me, motivate me, and inspire me. I did not attempt to move the mountains and accomplish great things, but I did realize in the early stages of loss how unhealthy it would be to dwell incessantly on the pain.

Sometimes, watching movies would help to give my mind a break. I chose films that had some sort of hero from whom I could draw strength; or, I would watch a funny movie or a musical. I would slip into the darkened theater, eat popcorn, sip a Coke, and dodge the pain for a couple of hours. This helped to renew my strength and to get my mind off of my problems and into the world of imagination and entertainment.

Magic of Melody

I also filled my life with music. It floated through the stereo system of my house and in my car. While listening to the heavenly music performed by the Atlanta Symphony Orchestra, I prayed that God would show how to make the remainder of my life on this earth a symphony.

At the age of 60, newly divorced and living alone, I knew that my life would never end as long as I stayed connected to the source of the universe—God. My life would become a symphony! My days, months, and years would become a song.

As the orchestra played, I noticed the places of rest in the music. Although there are no notes played during a rest in music, John Ruskin says that "there's the making of music in it." We can choose, in this season of life, to listen for the sound of music, even in the rests of loss and grief.

Art for the Heart

During that time of recovery, discovery, and reconstruction of my soul, I added art to my home. I bought William Hallmark's painting *The Scepter*, which depicts the Great Lion of Judah bedecked in a gown of gold, emerald, and pearl, and holding a royal scepter between His paws. Such royalty! The background Scripture of Jacob's blessing over Judah (see Genesis 49:8–10)—the inheritance all believers have in Christ—drew me into that same blessing, because, as a child of the King of Kings, I feel royal. All Christians belong to the royal family of God.

In another one of Hallmark's paintings, *The Bride of Christ*, a beautiful bride gazes out a window. A semblance of Jesus stands behind her, His loving hands on her shoulders. The painting reflects the purity of the bride of Christ—the church—and the Scripture beneath the painting reads, *"Let us rejoice and be glad and give the glory to Him, for the marriage of the Lamb has come and His bride has made herself ready"* (Revelation 19:7).

As I wrestled with the demise of my marriage, this painting and the accompanying Scripture reminded me, every time I passed it in the foyer, that Jesus is also my husband.

"For your Maker is your husband—the LORD Almighty is his name—the Holy One of Israel is your Redeemer; he is called the God of all the earth. The LORD will call you back as if you were a wife deserted and distressed in spirit—a wife who married young, only to be rejected," says your God. "For a brief moment I abandoned you, but with deep compassion I will bring you back." (Isaiah 54:5–7 NIV)

With the loss of my husband as the head of our household and our spiritual covering, I turned to Jesus.

COPING WITH LOSS THROUGH FORGIVENESS AND FREEDOM

Overcoming loss often requires forgiveness. Nothing ages us like unforgiveness, and nothing frees us like forgiving others—even those who have not apologized for hurting us!

Stop being mean, bad-tempered, and angry. Quarreling, harsh words, and dislike of others should have no place in your lives. Instead, be kind to each other, tenderhearted, forgiving one another, just as God has forgiven you because you belong to Christ. (Ephesians 4:31–32 TLB)

In some cases, the only way to be healed from loss is to forgive those who have wronged us. Remember, *"If you forgive men for their transgressions, your heavenly Father will also forgive you. But if you do not forgive men, then your Father will not forgive your transgressions"* (Matthew 6:14–15).

We all have sinned; we all need forgiveness. Remembering this truth makes it easier when it comes to forgiving anyone who has done us wrong, forgiving ourselves, and accepting God's forgiveness. God will renew us so that we can walk out of that loss, physically, mentally, socially, and spiritually. Forgiveness invigorates us. Life becomes sweeter when we rid ourselves of bitterness.

The Power of Gratitude

Miriam Kelm, whose husband died of cancer only a few years into their joyful marriage—the second for both of them—writes about the mystery of gratitude in prevailing over loss.

One of the books I read after George died compared the grief experience to riding a roller coaster blindfolded. It is a good analogy. You can just be going along, feeling fine, and then some tiny little thing—a comment, a smell, a piece of music—will trigger a memory that plunges you into the depths of inconsolable grief and loss. It is not an easy trip, even when you know time will be your ally in helping make the lows more bearable and the highs more frequent. "Right now" is all there is.

There was a stunning change when I began to just be thankful for the time I'd had with George. In my heart and in my prayers, I felt and expressed my gratitude. The prayers of gratitude brought me to a more peaceful acceptance of my awful loss. It seems to me that gratitude is a quite mysterious thing that, when offered in prayer, God uses as a bridge into our hearts and lives.

Somehow, gratitude changed the shape of my grief. I moved into closer relationship and listening to what God might have in mind and pondered again on the idea of an underlying purpose to the meeting and union of George and Miriam.

It takes time to work through our losses before we move into the stage of gratitude. But, once we are there, we can begin to seek God's plans for our future and the purpose behind our losses. After all these years of trusting God, He's proven repeatedly that His timing is perfect.

Listen to Your Dreams

Only God knew that the year 2000 would be the perfect pivot for my life. Knowing that I was in an emotional fog from the divorce, I asked my longtime friend and writing buddy, Jane Rubietta, to help me update the manuscript, even though she was 20 years younger. With passion and persistence, we honed the pages of *Fabulous After 50*. The book's first publication in 2000 launched me into a new life.

Shirley and Jane

Fabulous After 50 has opened many doors and opportunities to travel and speak. To God be the glory! Now, years after my divorce, my desire is to encourage other women to successfully navigate through the losses that are so prevalent in midlife.

Do you have a dream that you've been waiting for? We are propelled into victorious living as we move toward that dream, even though the wisps of grief have not entirely dissipated.

A Bedrock of Friendship

As we rebuild our lives in times of loss, we must recruit our close friends. I have cultivated a group of six intimate friends who support me, encourage me, and spend quality time with me. These friends have helped me prevail, as well as to embrace faith, hope, and happiness. To them, I'm not just some ex-wife, mother, or committee member; I am "just" myself.

A REAL CHANGE OF SCENERY

When the divorce was finalized, I needed a change of scenery to recover from the emotional trauma. I was thankful when my newfound lady friends invited me to visit New York City with their travel club.

During the trip, we laughed, shopped, attended Broadway plays, and experienced all the sounds and ambience of New York City. But, alone in my hotel room at night, I buried my face in the pillow and cried myself to sleep.

We may be far from finished in the grieving process, but seeking out new adventures, whether to far-flung places or to the local zoo or botanical garden, brings life back into our days. It shifts our focus from our own loss to the largeness of the world and to God's amazing creativity, giving us renewed energy for living well.

By doing the necessary "heart work" and using these prevailing strategies, we will navigate through our midlife loss with victory! Our aches will fade to joy, just as the dawn breaks through the night. After all, God has promised that when we walk through the waters, they will not overcome us. (See Isaiah 43:2.)

— • ● • —

"Through the struggles of life, I have the comfort of knowing that God loves me and will never leave me."
—Shirley W. Mitchell's Diary

— • ● • —

QUESTIONS FOR REFLECTION AND APPLICATION

1. What effects has loss had on your life?

2. How will you prevail over midlife loss in a positive way?

3. Where are you in the forgiveness process?

4. What steps will you take to recover from your loss, care for yourself, and rejoice in new life?

SEVEN SIMPLE SECRETS TO SURVIVING LOSS

1. While struggling in God's loving arms, feel the pain of loss.

2. Prevail. Make the best thing in your life out of the worse experience.

3. Experience the freedom of forgiveness.

4. Find your passion. Follow your bliss.

5. Focus on family, friends, music, art, and fun.

6. Forge a new track.

7. Rejoice in your new life.

LONGEVITY PROMISE

"Therefore we do not lose heart. Though outwardly we are wasting away, yet inwardly we are being renewed day by day. For our light and momentary troubles are achieving for us an eternal glory that far outweighs them all. So we fix our eyes not on what is seen, but on what is unseen. For what is seen is temporary, but what is unseen is eternal."
—2 Corinthians 4:16–18 (NIV)

Endnotes

1. Jane Rubietta, *Quiet Places: A Woman's Guide to Personal Retreat* (Minneapolis, MN: Bethany House Publishers, 1997), 59.

CHAPTER 8

CREATING YOUR SPACE

"Now, more than ever, people need their homes to be havens, because of everything that's gone on in the world."[1]
—Chris Madden

"No longer will they build houses and others live in them, or plant and others eat. For as the days of a tree, so will be the days of my people; my chosen ones will long enjoy the works of their hands."
—Isaiah 65:22 (NIV)

My spacious ranch home seemed entirely oversized for just one occupant. Yet, when I questioned if I should stay in the home we had built for the family in 1968, the Lord spoke Isaiah 54:2 to my heart: *"Enlarge the place of your tent, stretch your tent curtains wide, do not hold back; lengthen your cords, strengthen your stakes"* (NIV).

My children had grown up there. The halls rang with the sound of their laughter, their growing-up angst, their running feet, their fun and friends, their sleepless slumber parties. We all treasured those memories, and the children and grandchildren still enjoy returning for celebrations, visits, and holidays. For those reasons, after the divorce, I decided to stay there.

Motivated to keep the place in tip-top shape, I remodeled the home, one room at a time, as the inspiration came. I wanted to preserve the space where we had made so many good memories with family and friends, but I also knew that I needed to begin to shape it increasingly into a reflection of myself—my loves, my personality, my heart.

RENOVATING OUR INNER SELVES

As we age, we are often tempted to focus solely on remodeling the external reflections of ourselves—our homes, our wardrobes, our bodies—so much so that we forget that true beauty comes from within. We read in 1 Peter 3:3–4,

Your beauty should not come from outward adornment, such as braided hair and the wearing of jewelry and fine clothes. Instead, it should be that of your inner self, the unfading beauty of a gentle and quiet spirit, which is of great worth in God's sight. (NIV)

One of the reasons for this is that in America, we get it backward, concentrating first on our outer spaces. When we do this, we collapse because we're a hollow shell. For this reason, I want to discuss the importance of remodeling our inner space before we talk about remodeling our outer spaces.

Renovating the Heart

Remodeling a house that has become outmoded, inconvenient, and unserviceable adds zest to our lives. Our lives could be compared to our homes: As we become older and wiser, we realize that certain areas in ourselves need tearing out and rebuilding.

To build an addition on our home, the contractors must start with a strong foundation. Likewise, adding a "wing" to the structure of our interior lives requires a solid foundation of faith, hope, and love. Just as carpenters must tear out walls that have been eaten by termites or weakened with age in order to replace them, we must tear out the walls of busyness, mediocrity, and complacency in order to replace them with new materials: excellence, enthusiasm, and dedication.

When glass windows become cloudy with age, we replace them with new ones. Likewise, remodeling ourselves involves tearing out every negative "window" through which we viewed life—such as frustration, selfishness, anger, hate, and unforgiveness—and replacing each one with a new window, a fresh vantage point, of forgiveness, grace, and gratitude, which will allow the warm sunlight of God's love to beam inside.

Replacing the roof is one of the biggest remodeling projects there is. And so is the process of tearing off the old "shingles" of insecurity, fear, and hopelessness, and replacing them with a new covering of peace, patience, kindness, and goodness. It can make life feel new.

When we remodel a room, we make sure to polish the furniture that belongs in it, refurbishing and shining each piece, as needed. We may even decide to add a few new pieces. Similarly, as we age, we find ourselves at a time in our lives when we can, and must, refurbish, polish, and shine our old skills, as well as add new ones.

God, the Master Planner, has the power to remodel our again lives with beauty and charm. *"By wisdom a house is built, and through understanding it is established; through knowledge its rooms are filled with rare and beautiful treasures"* (Proverbs 24:3–4 NIV).

Fulfilling Lifelong Dreams

Jane's daughter, Ruthie, age 20, and son, Josh, age 13, stood in her kitchen one morning. Josh rubbed sleep from his eyes and said, "I had the best dream. I dreamt that the closet in the basement actually had another door, and when I opened that door, a whole new room was inside there, and it went on and on."

Ruthie smiled. "I love dreams like that."

Indeed. Dreams are full of creation, new life, and surprises; they reveal secrets and treasures we didn't know existed. And midlife is the time when many of our lifelong dreams can come true for us. In earlier years, we don't always take the time to act on our dreams. But, in midlife, when we find ourselves with more time on our hands, we may discover parts of ourselves we hadn't noticed before. We are able to redefine and redesign the "rooms" of our lives, to set aside time, space, and energy to consider how we want to alter our rooms, actual and symbolic, to reflect our character.

When I began to think about renovating my home, I knew that I had to incorporate comfort, as well as warm, rich, regal fabrics and fluidity of movement in the lines around me. When it came to my bedroom, I wanted cushiony comfort...and heaven! The Westin Hotel's "heavenly bed" inspired me, with its down comforters and feather pillows.

I also knew that I needed to begin my renovations by tending to my need for community. My first project was creating a magnificent patio in the backyard, which had once been a mud puddle. I was excited about this change and thrilled to host an open house and fund-raiser for my Business and Professional Women's Club on the new patio. My first party on the new patio was the means of providing scholarships for savvy young women who were working to get an education and pursuing a business degree. The bright, cheerful gala, which kicked off the Christmas season, helped my family to focus on charity during the holidays.

MAKING SPACE TO MEET YOUR NEEDS

The 60s season provides the perfect opportunity to make room for our new needs in midlife. We should ask ourselves: What are my spiritual needs in this decade? Physical? Relational? Creative?

Space for Spiritual Needs

I created a spiritual space for myself when I recreated my master bedroom. My decorator, Tom Warren, focused his designs on the rural beauty outside the bedroom and tastefully decorated a screened-in back porch. The antique wicker furniture and glowing ferns make for a perfect place to relax, sipping my morning cup of coffee and gazing out at the glorious countryside while listening to the birds. Having this space for morning devotions and prayer time is divine. In the peaceful seclusion of my back porch, I bring my hungry soul to God.

We all need a place to breathe alone, apart from the expectations formed by relationships. What does this look like, and how do we achieve this space? Jane awakens each morning before her husband and enjoys the solitude of their family room. The four windows in the room offer a view of the sloping lawn, with its towering oaks and lake. As the sun rises and the wind ripples the water like fairy footprints, Jane soaks in Scripture and stillness. The solitude and beauty fill her, preparing her for relationship with others and the work of the day.

Space for Physical Needs

Upon retiring, Louis and Betty found themselves tripping over each other. The sense of togetherness that they felt quickly staled. To bring life into their relationship again, they both decided to take turns going out alone in order to give each other time alone in the house. When they reunited at home, they had stories to tell of their time spent apart, bringing new life instead of cramped irritation into their marriage.

Space for Relational Needs

Fashioning a home that suits our needs is vital; finding friends who will call us into life, joy, and action is imperative, as well. When we have supportive friends, we are less likely to place unrealistic expectations on our family members, especially the expectation that they will magically discern what we need without our telling them. Good friends invite us into the fullness of who we are, challenge us to stop whining, and breathe adventure into our lives.

It has been my practice to surround myself with people of all ages who display qualities that I long to increase in myself: wit, intellect, sensitivity, grace, and wisdom. As I consider the bright faces of friends and family who help me grow, I am filled with gratitude.

Space for Creative Needs

As she neared retirement, Rhoda realized that she still longed for an outlet to express her creativity. She sectioned off a tiny spot in her basement, set up an easel, and now spends time regularly pouring her heart out onto canvas. Her husband understands that this is her time and her space.

When she and her husband downsized their home, Charlene created a nook off of the porch to serve as her sewing sanctuary. The walls are decorated with beautiful swatches of fabric, and a wooden rack displays colorful spools of thread. The coziness, the bright hues of cloth, and the solitude feed her as much as the projects she tackles there.

A SPACE TO CALL OUR OWN

Does it seem self-centered to renovate our inner and outer spaces? Why do we need to create our own space? The marketing committee at Faith Popcorn predicted that more and more people will be "cocooning," or living and working from their homes, in the years to come. Do you see this happening in your own life?

At first glance, "cocooning" may seem self-centered. Cocooning often means making your home a safe and fabulous place to work, shop, entertain, enjoy intimate times with your spouse, and host extended family for dinners, sleepovers, and holidays. It also provides personal space for quiet time. As Internet shopping, telecommuting, and self-employment become more popular patterns in our society, we can expect to see more and more "cocooning" in the future.

But, just as the tide sweeps in and then swooshes out, we also need a rhythm in our relationships—a rhythm where there's a coming together and a going apart. The going apart—the space—feeds our relationships. Designing that space—a place that is unique to each of us—is a lifelong task, particularly as we are considering who we will be for the next 30-plus years of our lives. We also need our living situation to reflect something of our inner selves. Our surrounding can shine the light on who we are and what we love.

For me, creating space helped me to deal with my divorce. It was also vital work as I began to consider who I would be for the rest of my life. Personal space creates a sanctuary, a safe place, a place of refuge, where we can relax from the demands made on us and the roles we must play; an area where we can focus and regroup. It is a place to be ourselves.

CREATING SPACE ON A BUDGET

You may be thinking, *But, Shirley, I don't have the money to renovate. My "dream house" would cost entirely too much.* The truth is, you can achieve a surprising amount on a shoestring budget.

The Clean Sweep

Perhaps the cheapest way to make space is to do a clean sweep. Creating space happens instantly when we go on a mission to get rid of clutter and streamline our belongings.

Dorothy was overwhelmed with the thought of organizing her office and creating a place to work that reflected who she was (rather than the chaos of her mind). She hired a personal coach, who told her about the "one-inch rule": Take a snapshot of the room and then focus on a one-inch-square space in the photo, sorting through what you can see in that space and either tossing it, giving it away, or putting it away. Then, stop and admire your progress before tackling the next inch, whether you do so tomorrow or next year.

When I began to revamp my personal space, I found that my collection was immense. The recreation room alone, which had been remodeled several before, was filled with everything we did not have a place for: furniture left over from college, sports equipment, and mementos from ball games, proms, and dances. You get the picture. The "rec room" was a wrecked room.

One woman said to me, "Just move. That helps to get rid of it all." The only problem is that in moving, you would give away all the memories, too. So, I made time to remember and celebrate as I sorted, and I gave cherished items to family members. I also found it helpful to select various charitable organizations that could benefit from my clean sweep. For instance, I donated some clothing to Job Corps, which provides clothing for women who are trying to get back into the workforce.

Getting rid of clutter accomplishes many things: it opens up our living space, simplifies cleaning and straightening (thus offering more time in our day for personal space), and allows us to see the walls and surfaces again. When my friend Kim reorganizes and refurbishes a room, she takes down the old pictures, gives them to her friends, and replaces them with new ones. When she finishes, the home feels transformed—and her only investment was in some picture hangers!

If a clean sweep is what your house needs, be sure to warn your husband! After Regina had cleaned out and rearranged her living room, her husband came home late from a meeting and, as was his habit, perched on the edge of the antique sewing machine. The only problem: she'd moved the sewing machine! He landed on the floor with a thump and a dazed look of surprise.

Creative Solutions

When I visited my friend Elizabeth, I noticed that she'd begun to decorate her living room and formal dining room with colors, fabrics, and objects that reflected an exotic side of her that I hadn't seen before. Her casual dining room had new colors, as well: soft yellow and royal blue. The colors were complemented by the love seat and pillows she had positioned under the window, the table runner, and the stack of gorgeous Fiestaware plates and bowls of assorted shapes and sizes.

"Beautiful, Elizabeth!" I exclaimed. "You've been on a mission. Where did you find this terrific collection?"

Her beaming smile warmed the room. "At the resale shop downtown. It's my favorite place to go when it's time to refurbish."

Another friend, Dorothy, purchased a townhome in a retirement community. When the construction began, she was eager to select pieces that would reflect her creativity. On a tight budget, she sorted through the shelves of a thrift store and selected several treasures to bring home. Remodeling is always an option, even for those who do not have a lot of money to spend!

When I saw my friend Carla last week, she showed me some pictures of her new home. She had transported some of the furniture from her previous home—gorgeous antiques she'd found "curbside shopping"—to her new space. She has become a whiz at refinishing furniture, and her home looked ready to be featured in a women's magazine.

Marlene was forced to downsize when she moved to a new home that afforded her no office space to work. Using an inexpensive but attractively carved folding partition, her friend helped her section off an alcove just inside the front door. A beautiful antique rocker, a kneeling bench, a small desk, a vase of fresh flowers, and an arrangement of her favorite books transformed the area into a sweet place to commune with God, meet with friends, and work. Her only purchase was that folding partition.

SACRIFICES OF CREATING SPACE

Creating or renovating our special spaces often involves sacrifice. But any sacrifice is well worth it!

When Creating Space Means Moving

Susan and Ken know that they will eventually need to downsize, not only for their own sakes, in terms of upkeep, but also to send the message to their adult children that they need to be independent from that point on. Years ago, Ken redid the entire home, inside and out, and part of him dies when he thinks of leaving his beautifully crafted, hand-carved woodwork, leaded-glass windows, and built-in desk and shelves.

Sometimes, we must downsize our personal space in order to accommodate new interests, different abilities, and limited energy levels. In these instances, we must allow ourselves to feel the loss of moving.

A friend of mine once said, "Don't try to do everything all at one time." She learned this after her husband retired and they moved to a new house they had built, all within a very short time span. Due to the move, they had to leave their church, their friends, and their community. Such extreme change sets off all sorts of imbalance alarms within us, and it calls for space. Again, we need space and time to grieve our losses and to heal. And we need the permission to take as long as we need in order to do so.

New Community

Sometimes, creating our space means moving to a new area, where we are anonymous in a sea of people. Teresa moved into a retirement community awhile ago. She did not know a single neighbor until a colleague recruited her to help generate support for a local youth center. Whereas before, she was hesitant to introduce herself to neighbors, she now found that knocking on door with a "purpose" opened many doors to relationships. She crossed the threshold of her comfort zone into a whole new territory. And as her friendships expanded, so did her energy.

When Jennifer and her husband retired, they built their dream home—the first house on the block. As other neighbors moved in, they kept to themselves. They were, as she said, "so independent. They all have their own lives and activities, and we are frustrated that we don't have many relationships here. In our former neighborhood, people chatted on the street, helped in a crisis, shared leftovers, and caught up on the latest news."

But resigning wasn't this woman's style. Too many people live lonely lives, and Jennifer loved having her home filled with people far too much to ignore this opportunity. God had gifted her with the ability to give people space to be themselves while in relationship with her. And she knew who she was well enough to take the first step.

To facilitate some community in the neighborhood, Jennifer organized a Christmas open house. In the invitations, she sent a card requesting personal information for each of the respondents to return to her, whether or not they attended the party. Many people did attend, and now Jennifer has a file of cards with information about the people in her little neighborhood—their family size, interests, and so on—which she can use for the next event she plans. As she considers the hopes, needs, and longings of her neighbors, she has found that these new friendships have inspired new areas of ministry for her.

As we create space for ourselves, we also get in touch with some of our delayed dreams—dreams that we have pushed aside while tending to the fullness of life in our younger years. Use those longings to propel you out of isolation and into special interest groups. Get involved in a church, a community service group, or a professional group.

Seek out a network of support as you pursue your dreams. For instance, my friend Verna said to me, "I've always wanted to write. I'm going to go to a writers' conference and meet some writers, then see if I can start a writers' group in my area."

MOTHER-DAUGHTER SPACE

An outstanding high school classmate of mine, who was always neat, organized, and productive, retired after a successful teaching career. She and her husband built a lovely home in a retirement community. The yard is always well-groomed, with beautiful seasonal flowers. Behind the home, they built a small house, adorned with window boxes of flowers, for her widowed mother. The arrangement afforded privacy to mother and daughter alike but was in close enough proximity that they shared companionship and a feeling of security.

As many women in their 60s begin to retire, they will also need to consider how to meet their parents' needs. This consideration provides an incentive to clean out your own space, so that you can be available to open up your house to family members in need.

IMAGINING YOUR PERFECT SPACE

Take the time to plan out what your space will look like. How will it reflect you and your personality? Brainstorm ideas for a new space that unleashes your creativity and gifts. Here are some suggestions:

- Describe your favorite setting, your "watering hole," the place that most feeds your soul. What do you love there? What nourishes you?

- Think of your favorite things and then list them. Your list might include Broadway plays, ballet shoes, a palette of paint, flowers, and silk fabrics. Do you enjoy plants? Tea? Candles? Crystal? Music? If so, what type of music?

- If you had a "trademark," what would it be? Fresh daisies? Vibrant colors? Dangly earrings?

- Imagine how a space of your own would look. What colors would you see? What would be on the walls? How would the furniture look? What music might you play?

Feel the fabric and texture of accessories in your new space; see the colors. Now, describe them.

- See yourself in this place. How do you feel here? What are you wearing? What is happening in your soul right now?

- What will it take to create space for yourself—space that reflects who you are, your deepest loves, your past, your future?

START NOW!

What type of setting do you prefer? It might be the seaside or a campsite; a country farmhouse or a mountain retreat; ruffles and froufrou or clean lines and sparse décor. Whatever your style, you can create a space that reflects your interests and personality. We cannot afford to live disconnected from our deepest longings during this season of our lives. Recreating our space will result in an integration of heart and soul, of inner and outer spaces, that will give grace to all who enter our homes and hearts.

Jane and I giggled and boo-hooed through the movie *Calendar Girls*, in which a group of women come together over a common grief. In the process of its resolution, they moved more fully into who they really were—their loves, interests, beauties—and created a whole new life for themselves, as well as for those around them, including those in their village.

We can do the same. Do not wait for the "perfect moment" to renovate your space; it will never come. Start now, little by little, and watch how God uses this transformation to bring life and joy to the world around you.

Sensational space—what a life-giving gesture!

———————————— • ● • ————————————

"A personal space, large or small, for nurturing the body,
soul, and mind, is a blessing for busy, multitasking women.
Where can I start in creating my space?"
—Shirley W. Mitchell's Diary

———————————— • ● • ————————————

QUESTIONS FOR REFLECTION AND APPLICATION

1. What is your dream for your own personal space? Dream in living color!

2. Be still and listen to your longings. What parts of your personality are longing to be released?

3. Write down some steps you must take to create that dream space. When will you take the first step?

SEVEN SECRETS TO CREATING SENSATIONAL SPACE

1. Know yourself.

2. Envision that perfect personal space. Rediscover lost loves and incorporate them here.

3. Allow your creativity to flow.

4. Make sure to allow for privacy in your new space.

5. Set aside time regularly to enjoy this space—even before it is finished.

6. Any place becomes personal space when we are quiet. Sit for 15 minutes, without an agenda, just listening to your heart and soul.

7. Invite God's presence to transform your time in your sanctuary.

LONGEVITY PROMISE

"Be still, and know that I am God."
—Psalm 46:10 (NIV)

Endnotes

1. Olivia Barker, "Chris Madden Has Comfort All Her Own," *USA Today* (24 September 2004): 7D.

CHAPTER 9

JOY RIDE: LIVIN' LIGHT, PHYSICALLY AND MENTALLY

"One must put all the happiness into each moment."
—Edith Wharton

"A joyful heart makes a cheerful face…
a cheerful heart has a continual feast."
—Proverbs 15:13, 15

A white convertible passed me on the road. The three women in the car wore red scarves around their necks that flew out behind them. They were laughing like crazy, clearly having fun.

The driver was my friend Carol Self, whom I had met at a Toastmasters International gathering years ago at the Mueller Company, a fire hydrant foundry, where she worked. My hometown sports a large gold fire hydrant in the lawn of the Chamber of Commerce with a sign that reads, "The Fire Hydrant Capital of the World."

When Carol bought the little white convertible, a Chrysler LeBaron, she lived on a farm and was the sole caretaker of the horses and cows. She had driven a three-quarter-ton truck for years, but this sensational-after-60 woman had always dreamed of driving a white convertible.

Carol told me, "I, along with a million other women, have always dreamed of going to the beach in a convertible, with a red scarf flying out behind me in the breeze. Yup! Why not? Yes, I did buy a convertible, and I am having the time of my life. I have gone to the beach, taken friends to lunch, and gone joyriding." Carol continued, "As we get older, we have to begin to do things for the pure joy of it and do some of the silly things we thought we might like to do when we were younger but never had the opportunity. We should always say to ourselves, 'If we don't do it today, we might not get to do it at all.' So let's open ourselves up to unlimited possibilities."

Carol added, "Memories that I have made in that little car have meant more to me than the money I paid for it. Little things like this—that one can still make happen—can make the later years of life more enjoyable and more fun."

Rather than living with regret—the "I wish I hads"—we, too, can smile because we dared to enter into our dreams. We live too short on joy and too long on complaints. We can lengthen our lives by doing things that bring joy and by learning how to lighten up. This includes taking care of our bodies, hearts, and minds, as well as our dreams.

Physical and mental fitness should be a top priority for women in their 60s. Here we will explore physical and mental health, along with the importance of humor in the life of the sensational-after-60 woman. One of the most encouraging truths I have learned about aging well is that we can *grow* until the time that we die.

But, to do this, we need a heart-to-heart conference about our bodies, our brains, and our outlooks on life. As my friend Jane tells women around the country when she speaks: "Age is inevitable; but maturity is optional." Let's go for the gold—a glowing self-assured maturity.

LIGHTEN UP, PHYSICALLY

Aging during the "Age Wave" is a high-seas adventure. Maybe you do not feel buoyant, but do not worry: There is still time to shed the weight of aging and join the women who are saying no to old and yes to life at any age.

Even as older women, we can choose to be characterized by youthfulness and vigor. As I watched an episode of *Oprah* that covered age-defying breakthroughs, I was convinced that this is the best time in history to be sensational after 60. At 50 years of age, Oprah said, "I'm selling 50. It's rejuvenating and exhilarating!" And she is still young, inside and out.

Oprah also said, "Doing what you love 'youngs' you up! Have a passion for what you do, and be with people you have a passion for. Take care of yourself first. If the well is empty, there is nothing to give out."

We can start by taking care of the "well"—our bodies.

AGING WELL

Total health is the result of a combination of good nutrition, physical activity, and other factors, such as getting adequate sleep, reducing stress, and meditating on Scriptures. When it comes to health, remember that small changes in habits can result in large benefits.

Reaching the sixth decade is a milestone. "Win-win" aging gives a sense of invincibility, power, and possibility. With regular exercise, proper diet, and a positive attitude, the aging generation can retard or repel the ravages of disease, time, and gravity.

These are the years to rekindle! Let's throw the word *retirement* out of our vocabulary. Exchange "old-timer" for "young-ager." Forget about being on your "last legs," and run forward to your golden years! Exercise until you change creaky and cranky into flexible and fun.

In regard to our health, and life in general, our fears are rarely fulfilled. "Only 10 percent of Americans 65 and over have a chronic health problem that restricts them from carrying on a major activity," one doctor told his patient.[1] He continued, "You need to make a body plan to keep everything up and running smoothly until the last years of your life." What will your body plan be?

Several years ago, Dr. Ken Dychtwald exhorted those who attended the Age Wave conference to live healthier, or else the United States would turn into one big nursing home. Regular exercise results in better health, giving us more strength, stamina, power, and energy. It puts a smile on our face and a spring in our step, no matter our age.

A fit body cannot be purchased, but it can be earned! It takes knowledge of nutrition and exercise, and it requires discipline, time, and hard work. Too often, we reap the results of poor self-care from our earlier years, and what we consider to be aging is actually disuse of our bodies.

Physical Activity with Dr. Debra Goodwin

Dr. Debra K. Goodwin, Ph.D., R.D., is Department Head and Associate
Professor in the Department of Family and Consumer Sciences at
Jacksonville State University, in Jacksonville, Alabama.
Her contributions to this chapter are greatly appreciated.

Physical activity is vital to a healthy lifestyle. Consequences
of inactivity often include cardiovascular disorders, type 2 diabetes, gallbladder disease, cancer, osteoporosis, obesity, sleepless-
ness, and cognitive disturbances. Therefore, it is important to
stay active and practice good nutrition.

Good fitness and health require combining adequate physical activity with good nutrition. Different types of activity provide different health benefits. This is why we should incorporate
many forms of activity into our exercise routine.

Here are some basic exercise guidelines, compiled from the
American College of Sports Medicine and from my sister Dr.
Debra Goodwin:

- Get at least one hour of moderate physical activity daily. Moderate exercise includes activities such as walking, golfing, gardening, and even completing household chores.

- Get at least 20 minutes of sustained aerobic activity three to five times per week. This may include brisk walking, biking, jogging, dancing, climbing stairs, or participating in an aerobics class.

- Complete 20 to 40 minutes of resistance training two to three times a week. Resistance training includes sit-ups, push-ups, and other weight training exercises. Local gyms often provide equipment for strength training, or you may choose to purchase your own.

- Complete daily stretch exercises. Overhead stretches and toe touches are among the simplest forms of stretch exercises.

Before undergoing any major increase in activity level, you should talk to your physician and, perhaps, a professional trainer, to make sure your body can withstand the extra stress. The major message here is to get moving. Remember to move correctly and safely.

Physical activity improves your metabolism, mood, memory, and stamina. It can also help you manage your weight, cholesterol, blood pressure, and sleep. Another benefit is that it can help strengthen your immunity, bones, and intestinal and respiratory function. Physical activity also decreases the risk of cardiovascular disease, certain types of cancer, and diabetes—good motivations to get going.

Don't dwindle—rekindle! Respark your life with daily exercise. You can do it! Helen Klein, age 81, started running at age 55, after her children were fully grown. She runs six or more marathons each year, finishing in under five hours every time, as well as ultramarathons (races at least 30 miles long). She says,

"We have so much potential we're not aware of until we push ourselves. And then we discover there really are no limits."[2]

Nancy walks before work every day; Teresa rides her bike four times a week and uses a stationary bike in inclement weather.

Someone once said that if you want to live longer, walk your dog; if you don't have a dog, walk it anyway. Midge walks all over town with her huge Labrador at a brisk pace, often for hours at a time. A caregiver for her husband, she spends her alone time walking her dog. The steady movement of aerobic exercise reduces stress, releases endorphins, creates feelings of well-being, stimulates creativity, and burns calories—not a bad return on 30 to 45 minutes of investment.

Can't keep a steady pace? Music helps us to direct our thoughts off the agony of exercise and impacts our minds. An Ohio State University study showed that "people who listened to classical music while working out on a treadmill scored higher on a verbal ability test than when they exercised without tunes."[3]

> It's never too late to commit...to exercise—and age and infirmity shouldn't stand in the way....A fitness director... recently designed a fitness regimen for 20 wheelchair-bound nonagenarians at a local nursing home. After 16 weeks of moderate strength training, 19 of the 20 were able to spend at least part of the day out of their wheelchairs. One was strong enough to live independently again... doctors and fitness experts say the message is obvious: Do whatever exercise you can, and get started right away.[4]

Exercise makes the most out of your best! Keep moving. Now is the perfect time to begin.

Own Your Health

For several years, Kathy has lived with dizziness and poor balance. Working as a teacher, she stands on her feet all day, and she makes sure to have something nearby to grab on to when she becomes dizzy. Her doctor prescribed her medication to control the symptoms. One day, her pharmacist said, "I'm sorry; your prescription cannot be refilled without seeing your doctor." Kathy could not get an appointment, and so she went without her medication.

The side effects eventually disappeared. The pressure in her head dissipated, along with the dizziness. When Kathy finally scheduled an appointment, the doctor looked at her in surprise. "You've changed. What's different about you?"

"I'm alive again," Kathy said. She placed her pill bottles in her doctor's lap. "I quit taking these meds. My blood pressure is normal. My dizziness is gone." Her husband could not believe the difference. Kathy's energy level skyrocketed, and she now finishes her sentences without losing her train of thought. She feels great!

Make sure that you talk about the side effects of your medications with your primary care physician and pharmacist. Ask them about the possibility of lowering your doses and about the potential side effects. Request the drug package inserts from your pharmacist, which provide more reliable information than what you may find on the Internet. Ask questions. We must take responsibility for our own health. We know ourselves best. Doctors want the best for us, but cannot possibly know ourselves as well as we do.

CARING FOR THE OUTWARD APPEARANCE

Now that we're tuning up the engine and taking care of our health, let us consider some external fixer-uppers for the sensational-after-60 woman.

Skin

The sixth decade gave me a new challenge: moisturizing! If I do not moisturize my lips with Burt's Beeswax Lip Balm, they become so dry that they crack open. It's really important that we moisturize our skin. Select bath products, lotions, and makeup with hydrating properties to give your skin a healthy, youthful glow.

Hair

I enjoyed watching *The Promise*, a musical production by the Promise Entertainment Group, at a theater in Branson, Missouri. I was amazed at the large number of hoary heads I observed in the audience. The healthy, shiny white hairstyles of the mature women certainly added to their radiance. They gleamed in the crowd, reminding me of Proverbs 16:31: *"The hoary head is a crown of glory, if it be found in the way of righteousness"* (KJV).

One of the problems we may encounter as we age is thinning hair. This may be a good time for you to consult a professional hairdresser who will help change your hair style, give advice on what shampoo and conditioner to use, or give you a special cut that will enhance volume. My friend Sandra Benefield is a beautiful over-60 woman who has a haircut that complements her face, and she proudly wears her crown of glory.

Friend Sandra Benefield with hairdresser Michael King

Some women choose to have their hair professionally colored with shades that complement their skin tones. Others may decide to experiment with different colors at home. A box of hair color may open up a new chapter in your life or personality!

Another problem we encounter as we age is that our hairstyles do not grow up with us. The long hair of our youth may not be the best style for our sexy 60s! Although it may hide our aging necks, it may also draw our face down into long, tired lines.

In general, a hairstyle should frame our face—like a gorgeous picture frame—without duplicating its shape. Following one of the rules for clothing, we never want to end a line at our widest point, because that will create emphasis. An oval face is complemented by an angled haircut. Angles are also slimming on a round face, while a spherical cap of curls will emphasize the roundness. A wide forehead will tend to look even wider with bangs but will look minimized with wisps of hair or hair that is swept to the side.

Shirley with Michael

Whether we cut or curl, color or go natural, our hair can be our crowning glory at this time in our lives—and we don't have to spend a lot of time or money on it. Because we represent the Creator, we work toward showing forth His excellence.

Teeth

Gail, a late-in-life mom, was in her 50s when her daughter got braces. She was thrilled for her, but she refused to think about getting them for herself, even though she always covered her mouth when smiling. After all, should she care what others think about her teeth?

Dr. Paul Kattner, D.D.S., M.S., of Waukegan, Illinois, says that midlife women come into his office for braces daily. And why not? They may have 30 to 40 more years of life. Why not "smile at the days to come" with teeth you feel good about displaying?

Many women are taking advantage of orthodontic treatments in their later years. After Jane's two children had their smiles perfected, she learned that she had malocclusion (a bad bite) herself, so she decided to get braces. She was in her 40s. Now, when she sees a woman with braces, she asks her, "Why did you get them?" One woman summed it up perfectly. She didn't care what others thought. "Because when I looked in the mirror, that wasn't who I was."

THE MIND: USE IT OR LOSE IT

The more alive we are, the better connections are made in our brains. Expanding our horizons strengthens our brains. A characteristic that many centenarians share, for instance, is an open mind about life and its issues, as well as a certain wonder in their regard for life.

Experts believe that there is no significant loss of cognitive ability before the ages of 60 to 65. In fact, the "use it or lose it" rule applies to our brain, as well. Even in our 60s, the mind can still learn, grow, and expand. "Cognitive skill is similar to driving skill: Even though reaction time slows, performance can be maintained—even improved—by practicing, using brain circuits, and keeping them busy."[5]

One spin-off from the famous "Nun Study" in the 1990s examined nuns "carefully chosen for similar lifestyles, but [had] differences in educational level....Despite the equivalence in adult lifestyle, highly educated nuns were twice as likely to avoid Alzheimer's and other dementias late in life than less educated nuns."[6] Another study found that "mice that exercised regularly on a running wheel grew twice as many new brain cells as other mice."[7]

Keeping our minds limber actually helps to stave off the effects of old age. The more we know, the more we grow!

LIGHTNESS OF HEART

Not only do some of us carry too much physical weight, but we also lug around too much emotional weight. We take life too seriously; everything is a potential for crisis. And we create problems for ourselves by not aging outside the box—choosing to move beyond the barriers we (and others) create for ourselves. Instead, we let others define how we age. But there are ways of avoiding this.

Laugh and Last

One of the ways to lighten up is to laugh more. Experts say that a healthy child laughs 100 a day; most adults barely make it to the 15 mark. Helen's mother is 80, but her grandkids don't see her as "old." Why not? "Grandma laughs a lot."

Rent a funny movie, read a daily "clean joke" on the Internet, or exchange funny stories with others. If you still can't laugh, purchase a laugh track and see if you don't get healthier by the chuckle.

We always get to choose how to respond to events in life. Laughing will keep us young.

Journaling

Journaling is another way to lighten up. In her beautifully written and illustrated book *Love Letters to God*, Lynn Morrissey shared that journaling was not only an avenue to healing and understanding God's heart; it also helped replace the sorrow in her life with joy.

As I "spoke sorrow" in prayer in my journal, something astonishing occurred: I was gradually being transformed. My heartbreak quietly, slowly, at first imperceptibly, began breaking into joy.... Although still feeling the pain of life's losses, I was no longer despondent. Instead, I was deepened by what I'd gained.[8]

Reconciliation

We haul around other weights that age us, like bitterness and unforgiveness. Reconciling broken relationships is vital in this stage of our race. It is important to forgive, regardless of whether the person forgives us or is sorry for causing the pain. This is the time to accept the fact that we have had an imperfect past, imperfect parents, and imperfect people in our lives—and that we have been imperfect, as well.

Reconciliation forces us to stop blaming and to move fully into who we are and where we are *now*, not how we got there. The question is not "Who hurt me along the way?" but rather "How will I live from here on out?"

Is it too late to start over in relationships? Never!

We do not have to be anyone else's idea of successful at 60. We do not have to be superhuman for another second. We are free to make mistakes, to be imperfect, and to ask for help when necessary.

This is the best time in life. Having survived disease and accidents and all of the curveballs that life throws our way, we have more time at 60 and beyond for leisure, freedom, family, friendships, and growing in wisdom. We can choose to lighten up and get younger by the minute!

—————————— • ● • ——————————

"Rejoicing takes the friction out of aging."
—Shirley W. Mitchell's Diary

—————————— • ● • ——————————

QUESTIONS FOR REFLECTION AND APPLICATION

1. What is your body plan? How do you want to be in your eighties? Start planning for it now!

2. List your primary health questions and concerns. How will you be proactive about your health?

3. When it comes to living light, in what areas do you most need to lighten up? What will that look like for you? Reconciliation? Asking for help? Journaling?

AUDREY HEPBURN'S SEVEN SIMPLE "BEAUTY TIPS"[9]

1. For attractive lips, speak words of kindness.

2. For lovely eyes, seek out the good in people.

3. For a slim figure, share your food with the hungry.

4. For beautiful hair, let a child run his or her fingers through it once a day.

5. For poise, walk with the knowledge that you will never walk alone.

6. People, even more than things, have to be restored, renewed, revived, reclaimed, and redeemed; never throw out anybody.

7. Remember, if you ever need a helping hand, you'll find one at the end of your arm. As you grow older, you will discover that you have two hands: one for helping yourself, and the other for helping others.

LONGEVITY PROMISE

"The wise in heart are called discerning, and pleasant words promote instruction. Understanding is a fountain of life to those who have it....Pleasant words are a honeycomb, sweet to the soul and healing to the bones."
—Proverbs 16:21–22, 24 (NIV)

Endnotes

1. Gail Sheehy, New Passages: Mapping Your Life Across Time (New York, NY: Ballantine Books, 1995), 351.

2. Tish Hamilton, "In the Running," More (September 2004): 154.

3. Kathleen McAuliffe, "Health News," More (September 2004): 140.

4. Ellen Licking, "Workouts—Without the Work," Bloomberg Businessweek, http://www.businessweek.com/ stories/2004-08-29/online-extra-workouts-without-the-work.

5. Allen D. Bragdon and David Gamon, Ph.D., *Use It or Lose It!: How to Keep Your Brain Fit as It Ages* (New York, NY: Walker and Co., 2003), 3.

6. Ibid., 105.

7. Ibid., 101.

8. Lynn Morrissey, *Love Letters to God* (Sisters, OR: Multnomah Publishers, 2004), 30–31.

9. Sam Levenson, "Time Tested Beauty Tips," *In One Era and out the Other* (New York, NY: Simon & Schuster, 1973). This was Audrey Hepburn's favorite poem.

CHAPTER 10

MENOPAUSE, MEDICATIONS, AND MORE: QUESTIONS WOMEN ASK THEIR DOCTORS

"A joyful heart is good medicine."
—Proverbs 17:22

Health is a major concern for women who are approaching or are in their 60s. In this chapter, my favorite gynecologist, Dr. James Upchurch of Birmingham, Alabama, offers answers to some of the top health questions women ask in their 60s.

Shirley: What are some of women's health concerns as they go through their sixth decade?

Dr. Upchurch: Cardiovascular disease is the main concern. Approximately 500,000 women die each year of cardiovascular disease in the United States—over 40 percent of all female deaths in a given year. Coronary artery disease accounts for the majority of women who die of cardiovascular disease. Cancer is the second most common cause of death, followed by stroke, then chronic lower respiratory diseases, kidney disease, Alzheimer's disease, diabetes, influenza, and septicemia (severe blood infection).

A few years ago, a study by Stanford University showed that the majority of the women did not know that cardiovascular disease was the leading cause of death in women. Lung cancer is the greatest killer in women between the ages of 55 and 75. Breast cancer is the number one killer between the ages of 45 and 54, and colon cancer is the number one killer above 75.

Other common issues in the sixth decade are obesity, arthritis, thyroid disease, and neurological and psychological disorders. Sexual dysfunction due to vaginal dryness, absence or disease of orgasmic response, and intercourse pain are common disorders. Osteoporosis is certainly one of the more significant problems that the medical community deals with in the sixth decade.

Shirley: Could you discuss osteoporosis in a little more detail?

Dr. Upchurch: Osteoporosis can be diagnosed and fracture risk can be calculated using various techniques for measuring bone density. The gold standard for this measurement is known as a DEXA scan (dual energy X-ray absorptiometry). Osteoporosis is characterized by bones that have lost large amounts of calcium and will fracture more easily from physical activity or injury.

When we measure the bone density of a patient, the report comes back normal, or reveals osteopenia or osteoporosis, and the specific measurement of bone loss will be reported by the radiologist.

The patient with osteopenia has bone loss, but not such that she is in the osteoporosis category at the time of the DEXA scan. However, patients with osteopenia are subject to fractures and, in severe cases, should be treated to prevent upcoming osteoporosis.

Shirley: What are some treatments for osteopenia and osteoporosis?

Dr. Upchurch: Women in the sixth decade should take 1,500 mg of calcium per day, with 400 to 600 international units per day of vitamin D. Estrogens with or without progesterone have been shown to be a very effective medication to reduce the risk of all types of bone fractures, such as hip and back. The FDA has also approved Raloxifene, disphosphonates, and the hormones calcitonin and teriparatide for the treatment of osteoporosis. Disphosphonates typically are taken once a week on an empty stomach with a lot of water. The patient is not to eat anything or lie down for 30 minutes. Calcitonin is used as a nasal spray. Raloxifene is taken orally on a daily basis and is approved for prevention and treatment of osteoporosis by the FDA. It can cause hot flashes, night sweats, and muscular pains, so not every patient should take this drug. Raloxifene has also been found to reduce the risk of breast cancer significantly. Teriparatide is an expensive daily injection, but it greatly reduces the risk of osteoporosis and fractures.

Shirley: What predisposes patients to osteoporosis?

Dr. Upchurch: Osteoporosis is much more common in women and becomes more severe as the patient's age progresses. It is more common in Caucasians and is especially prevalent in women who have a family history of osteoporosis. Smoking, low body weight, poor calcium and vitamin D intake, and inadequate physical activity contribute to osteoporosis. Certain drugs, such as steroids, increase the risk of osteoporosis.

If a patient takes hormone replacement therapy (HRT) and discontinues it for any reason, she will have accelerated bone loss for as much as four to six years after discontinuing estrogen. Discontinuing estrogen then allows for fracture rates to increase. If a patient decides she does not want to restart her hormone replacement therapy, then she should be placed on some alternative treatment to protect her bones. Calcium and vitamin D alone will not accomplish that, but the addition of a drug such as Raloxifene will solve the problem.

Shirley: Should women take estrogen in their 60s?

Dr. Upchurch: Some physicians would say that patients in their 60s should not take hormones. Others would say that women who are taking hormones in their 60s should taper off and stop treatment as soon as they can overcome the hot flashes and night sweats. Another group would say that long-term HRT is acceptable for some women who have no health contraindications and are aware of all its risks and benefits. Each patient is unique, and the physician must determine what is best for each individual.

Some patients discontinue HRT and find that hot flashes and night sweats become intolerable. I believe it is acceptable to put these patients back on HRT after a failed attempt to withdraw if they are completely aware of the risks and benefits of restarting the hormone therapy. Some women in their 60s who cannot take one of the bone-building medications because of its side effects need to consider estrogen because of its fracture-reducing benefit.

Some patients stop taking estrogen with no side effects whatsoever. In my private practice, I encourage these women to continue taking calcium and vitamin D. I suggest Raloxifene if the patient does not have osteoporosis because it will stop the acceleration of bone loss. If osteoporosis is present, I prescribe one of the drugs we have already discussed.

Women desiring more information on this subject should look at the findings of the Women's Health Initiative (WHI) study on the Internet. However, I believe that the North American Menopause Society's Web site offers the most complete view on HRT. They have issued a learned report for each of the last several years, which includes their recommendations for estrogen and progesterone use. The experts who authored these reports used not only the WHI information but also all the pertinent journal articles that had been written in the past few years.

Shirley: Are there any increased risks if hormones are taken between the ages of 60 and 70?

Dr. Upchurch: The WHI study generated much publicity about this subject. One group of women in the study took no hormones whatsoever. Another group took conjugated equine estrogen (CEE) only, and another group took estrogen (CEE) and a progesterone-type compound (progestin). The results of the estrogen-progestin arm of the study and the estrogen study were very similar, with the exception of breast cancer. In the estrogen-only arm of the study, there was a decrease in cases of breast cancer. I don't recall seeing a single report on TV or in the newspaper about that fact. There was a slight increase in the number of heart-attacks, strokes, and phlebitis in women who took hormones in the study over the women who took no hormones. Breast cancer was slightly increased in the arm of the study where estrogen and progestin were taken together.

There was a small increase in cases of dementia in women over 75 who had taken hormone therapy for a few years. I do not know any gynecologists who would start HRT for the first time in women over 60, and no clinician should expect any improvement in the mental condition of this group due to HRT.

This study certainly has its critics and some of the data can be misleading. For example, the study indicated an increased rate of heart attack in hormone takers, but only the women who were 20 or more years past their menopause when they started their hormones had any significant increase in coronary heart disease.

Shirley: What do you think about hormone preparations that are compounded by some pharmacies?

Dr. Upchurch: The popularity for compounded HRT has been increasing. Many women seem to think that these drugs are perfectly safe, but the truth is that the same risks and benefits that I have already discussed also apply to these compounds.

Shirley: What can a woman do to improve her chances of better health in the sixth decade?

Dr. Upchurch: We can go right back to the basics of proper diet, exercise, vitamins, calcium, and regular medical checkups. In addition to regular gynecological examinations, the patient should have an annual battery of blood tests to check her cholesterol, blood sugar, thyroid, and so forth. Appropriate medications for elevated cholesterol, diabetes, high blood pressure, and other chronic diseases should be used faithfully by the patient. She should also undergo a DEXA scan to check for osteoporosis. Much evaluation has taken place on the benefits of low-dose and even ultra-low-dose estrogen therapy on the postmenopausal patient. The results were that very low doses of estrogen can provide relief from menopausal symptoms, as well as protect bone density. In the future, the dosage recommendation may drop significantly.

New drugs are on the horizon, and I look forward to the opportunity to use them once their safety has been established.

Shirley: Dr. Upchurch, it's good to know that there is hope for maintaining good health after menopause, but can women still be sexy after 60? What happens to a woman's sexual desire in the sixth decade?

Dr. Upchurch: In the 60s, women experience a new liberty: no fear of pregnancy or of being interrupted by children running into the bedroom, and less professional stress. This freedom may coincide with a drop in libido, or sexual desire. Women in their 60s can certainly be desirable and sexy, and sex can be better than ever. However, because each woman is so different, each one will experience this scenario in a different way. So much depends on the woman's spiritual maturity, physical health, mental status, and self-esteem. The same is true for her husband. Erectile dysfunction (ED) may cause men to be less attentive to their wives. Also, testosterone levels can drop so low in men that they have no interest in intimacy or even a desire to use ED treatments. The wife may read her husband's disinterest as a lack of attraction, internalizing it as her fault. Frank and honest communication between both individuals can help immensely.

Sexual libido can diminish significantly in women because of hormone imbalance. Estrogen helps with sensitivity and vaginal lubrication, but androgens (male hormones) are thought to be the source of women's sexual libido. The ovaries and adrenal glands produce androgens, but aging and ovary removal reduce the amount of circulating androgens. Physicians can prescribe androgens for libido problems, but, in my experience, increased libido usually requires a higher dose than I like to prescribe. These higher doses may cause mood changes, increased facial hair, and acne. Cholesterol and triglyceride levels can also be adversely affected by androgens. Low doses of androgen medication increase libido in some women, so prescribing androgens is acceptable if close follow-up is provided.

With proper attention and care, sex after 60 can be good—even better!

Shirley: Thank you, Dr. Upchurch, for your wisdom and concern, and for helping women to be sensational-over-60!

• ● •

"There is no reason to fear the 60s.
These can be prime years when we take care of our bodies,
our souls, and our minds!"
—Shirley W. Mitchell's Diary

• ● •

QUESTIONS FOR REFLECTION AND APPLICATION

1. What is your greatest fear about aging when it comes to your own health?

2. What is the health history of the women in your family? Consider the top health concerns facing women: cardiovascular diseases, stroke, diabetes, respiratory issues, and so on.

3. How are you currently caring for your physical well-being? How does this coordinate with your aging goals? In what areas can you improve your self-care?

SEVEN SIMPLE STEPS TO HEALTH

1. Schedule an annual physical.

2. Write out your "optimal aging plan" and share it with your doctor.

3. Schedule annual tests to check your cholesterol, blood sugar, thyroid, and bone density.

4. Bring all of your medications to your next doctor's appointment and discuss the questions and/or concerns that you have about them.

5. Make a health family tree. Include any diseases or health problems in your family line.

6. Ask a spouse, friend, or other loved one to go with you to the doctor if you find it difficult to get all the facts down or to ask questions.

7. Know yourself. Trust your body and your inner voice when it comes to asking questions and finding answers.

LONGEVITY PROMISE

"He will renew your life and sustain you in your old age."
—Ruth 4:15 (NIV)

CHAPTER 11

HEALTHY BY CHOICE,
NOT BY CHANCE
with Dr. Debra Goodwin

"I'm on the metric diet....You just buy a scale that measures your weight in metric. You can eat whatever you want and never break 100. Extra weight and middle age just seem to go together. We wake up one morning and discover we're retaining more water than Atlantis."[1]
—Comedian Martha Bolton

"Whether, then, you eat or drink or whatever you do, do all to the glory of God."
—1 Corinthians 10:31

Molly is one of the most sensational-after-60 women I know. A vibrant mother of two and a grandmother of four, she still works full-time, is active in church, and supports all those for whom she cares by attending their ball games, weddings, birthday parties, graduations, and other events. Molly has always been tall, lean, and energetic.

But, as with most women, she noticed subtle changes in her body after she turned 60. Her body composition changed somewhat, her normally small waist grew a proverbial "spare tire," and her stamina declined.

Not one to accept what she could change, Molly chose to take a healthier approach to life. She researched current dietary suggestions and reduced the amount of simple carbohydrates she consumed—particularly white bread, white potatoes, and sugar. She also started eating small, sensible snacks between meals to stave off the "munchies."

To enhance this healthier approach, she increased her walking by making small changes to her routine, such choosing the parking spot farthest from the building, delivering mail to the main office instead of using interoffice mail, and taking the stairs more often. These simple changes in diet and activity helped her to lose 20 pounds in less than eight weeks. She also had more energy.

Health is a matter of choice, not chance. Seek credible sources for health information and apply it wisely in your quest for a healthy lifestyle. Media messages regarding health may overwhelm or intimidate, but sensational-after-60 women who find themselves in the same dilemma as Molly should take heart. Small lifestyle changes in diet and exercise can help you reap large benefits.

DIET AND HEALTH

"Let food be your medicine and medicine be your food."
—Hippocrates, 400 B.C.

Good nutrition is a cornerstone of good health. Sensational-after-60 women should be aware of their nutritional needs and how to meet them. Women should be familiar with the role that calcium, fiber, sugar, fats, fruits, vegetables, and water play in their diets. They should also try to vary their diet, so that they get the important nutrients and minerals that they need.

Follow the Food Plate

In 2012, the USDA replaced the traditional food pyramid with the new food plate—a visual representation of the daily foods that individuals should eat for good health. Three-fourths of the plate should consist in plant-based foods, such as fruits, vegetables, and grains products (such as bread, pasta, and cereals). The remaining fourth of the plate contains low-fat proteins, such as meat, poultry, fish, and dried beans or peas. Dairy products, such as milk, cheese, and yogurt, are represented by a smaller plate on the side. The emphasis of the new food plate is a balanced diet through consumption of more plant-based foods and smaller portions.

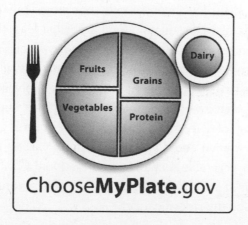

Whole-grain breads, brown rice, cereals, and pastas provide valuable B-complex vitamins and minerals, plus a lot of fiber. For most women in their 60s, six servings would meet their daily nutritional needs. Seem like too much? Don't confuse "servings"

with "helpings." One slice of bread; half a cup of rice, pasta, or cooked cereal; or one cup of ready-to-eat cereal constitute one serving. A sample daily intake of grains might include one cup of ready-to-eat cereal, two slices of whole-grain bread, half a cup brown rice, and one cup of pasta.

Fruits are also important, because they provide vitamin C, beta-carotene, fiber, and other minerals. Women need between two to three servings of fruit each day. Choices might include a medium apple, banana, orange, or pear; half a cup chopped fresh, cooked, or canned fruit; or three-fourths a cup of fruit juice. Moderately active women could meet their daily fruit needs with three-fourths a cup of orange juice and one banana. Very active women could add an apple or a pear to equal three servings.

Vegetables provide most of the same basic nutrients as fruits. However, since fruits contain more natural sugars and therefore more calories, vegetables are a good alternative at times because they are excellent low-calorie foods that provide many vitamins and minerals, as well as fiber. Women need at least three to four servings of vegetables daily. Diet options may include half a cup cooked green beans, peas, or carrots; one cup leafy green vegetables, such as lettuce or spinach; or a quarter cup vegetable juice. Moderately active women could add a quarter cup of tomato juice, one cup of leafy greens, and a quarter cup of green beans. Very active women could add half a cup of carrots to their diet to total four vegetable servings. The National Cancer Institute recommends at least five to nine servings of fruits and vegetables to help reduce the risk of cancer.

With two-thirds of our diet coming from plant-based foods, the remaining one-third should consist of meat alternatives and dairy products. Women need two servings (3 oz. each) of lean meat, poultry, fish, or other alternatives daily. This food group provides protein, iron, and important B-complex vitamins. Of course, high-fat meats, such as fried meats and steak, should be avoided when possible. (See the recipe section at the end of this chapter for more about portion sizes and preparation styles.) In addition, we also need at least three servings of dairy products a day. Dairy provides calcium, protein, and other important vitamins.

Calcium

Although the sensational-after-60 woman is no longer growing physically, her need for calcium to maintain strong bones and teeth continues. Unfortunately, national statistics reveal that 50 percent of women do not get the recommended daily 1,200 mg of calcium. Skipping milk affects more than just bones. Studies also indicate that adequate calcium intake may help maintain proper weight. Including calcium in daily diet is crucial for our 60s to be sensational.

Calcium may be obtained from a variety of foods. With a few wise choices, women can increase their calcium intake relatively easily. To add calcium-rich foods to your diet...

* use low-fat milk with your cereal.
* drink calcium-fortified soy milk.
* top mixed fresh fruit with low-fat cottage cheese or yogurt.
* top salads or casseroles with low-fat cheddar cheese.
* stuff celery sticks with low-fat mozzarella cheese.
* add low-fat cream cheese to cooked vegetables, such as spinach.
* add garbanzo beans (chickpeas) to salads.
* consume plenty of broccoli, spinach, and other leafy greens.

- choose low-fat ice creams or puddings for dessert.

- eat canned salmon or sardines (containing small bones).

Check out these sample menus to see how easily calcium can be added to your daily diet:

Breakfast   *Calcium*

2 slices whole-wheat toast......................................50 mg

2 oz. low-fat cheddar cheese ....400 mg

1 cup (8 oz.) low-fat milk.....................................300 mg

Snack

1 cup fresh fruit with 1/2 cup
lemon-flavored low-fat yogurt .... 125 mg

Lunch

Tossed salad topped with:

1/2 cup low-fat cottage cheese .... 75 mg

1/2 cup garbanzo beans ....40 mg

1/2 cup shredded low-fat cheddar cheese .... 100 mg

3/4 cup raw broccoli ....50 mg

Snack

Celery sticks with 1 oz. low-fat
mozzarella cheese ....200 mg

Dinner

1/2 cup salmon salad (canned salmon with
bones, low-fat mayo, and chopped boiled eggs

served on bed of lettuce with raw
vegetables and crackers) .... 275 mg

1/2 cup low-fat pudding .... 150 mg

1,765 mg

Knowledge is power. And knowing the amount of calcium in different foods can help the sensational-after-60 woman plan a powerful, calcium-rich diet to protect those beautiful bones.

Fiber

As with calcium, fiber may be one of the most important nutrients that are overlooked when planning a diet. Fiber, also known as roughage and bulk, is the indigestible portion of plant products. Adequate fiber consumption yields important benefits, including good colon health, decreased cholesterol levels, and weight management.

According to national health statistics, Americans, in general, consume less than half of the daily recommended 25 to 35 grams of fiber. This could be because the food sources that are high in fiber are not well-known. It always surprises people to learn that one slice of white bread contains .5 grams of fiber, whereas one slice of whole-grain bread provides 2 to 3 grams of fiber. Dried beans and peas, such as pinto beans and black-eyed peas, contribute a lion's share of fiber, with up to 12 grams per cup.

Meet daily fiber requirements with high-fiber foods, such as those listed on the following menu:

Breakfast   *Fiber*

1 cup whole-grain cereal (such as
shredded wheat with low-fat milk) .... 4 grams

Lunch   *Fiber*

Tossed salad (with lettuce, green peppers,
tomatoes, raw broccoli, garbanzo beans) .... 12 grams

ground wheat crackers (5) .... 2 grams

Dinner

1 cup pinto beans (dried) .... 12 grams

1 cup steamed cabbage .... 3 grams
                                                        ─────────
                                                        33 grams

Consuming adequate fiber is definitely a matter of choice, not chance. Getting enough fiber in the diet will help boost the sensational-after-60 woman's health.

Sugar

Conquering a "sweet tooth" may be problematic for many of us. The average American consumes more than 150 pounds of sugar annually. That's the equivalent to 30 five-pound bags of sugar each year! Excess sugar often means excess calories and weight gain. According to the World Health Organization, less than 10 percent of our total calories should come from sugar.

For many of us, reducing the sugar in our diets requires new habits. Consume soft drinks, candies, cookies, cakes, and desserts in small amounts. Satisfy those sugar cravings with naturally sweet foods, such as fruits.

Try this on for size: A 12-ounce soft drink alone contains up to 9 teaspoons sugar. If a woman who drinks one regular soft drink a day stops the habit, she cuts out approximately 140 calories per day, 980 calories per week, 3,920 per month, and 47,040 per year! Theoretically, this will bring about a weight loss of approximately 13 pounds in one year—just by drinking one less soft drink a day!

Fruits and Vegetables

As I mentioned earlier, fruits and vegetables provide valuable vitamins and minerals, as well as fiber. These colorful and tasty plant foods also provide phytochemicals and antioxidants, which improve the body's ability to fight and prevent diseases— another important reason to consume five to nine servings of fruits and vegetables daily.

To give you an idea of the importance of eating fresh fruits and vegetables, here is a list of some phytochemicals with their potential health benefits, as outlined by Food and Health Communications, Inc.:

- Allyl sulfides, found in onions, garlic, and leeks, protect against cancer-causing chemicals, as well as heart disease.

- Beta-carotene, found in dark orange and green fruits and vegetables, reduces the risk of cancer and improves the immune system.

- Lutein, found in summer squash and dark green, leafy vegetables, such as spinach, protects the retina of the eye.

- Lycopene, found in tomatoes, red peppers, and watermelon, decreases the risk of cancer.

- Isothiocyanates, found in broccoli, boost the body's natural immunity against cancer.

- Flavonoids, found in berries, cherries, apples, black and green tea, and red wine, increase levels of good cholesterol (HDL), protect against cancer, and have anti-inflammatory properties, as well.

The good news is that we consume phytochemicals by eating the recommended amounts of fruits, vegetables, and whole-grain products. We can also do this by keeping fruits and vegetables readily available to eat as snacks.

Fat

Because of our "fatophobic" society, the mere mention of the word "fat" brings negative connotations. For all of its bad press, fat has its benefits: it supplies energy, supports cell walls, and digests the fat-soluble vitamins A, D, E, and K. It also provides essential fatty acids.

Fat should make up no more than 30 percent of our total caloric intake. Animal fat is the least healthy because it tends to increase cholesterol in the body, so we should limit our consumption of high-fat meats and dairy products. To get the essential nutrients from meat and dairy, choose the low-fat versions of these foods.

The fats in plant products tend to help decrease cholesterol. These fats are found in olive oil, canola oil, peanut oil, flaxseed, salmon, mackerel, tuna, shellfish, walnuts, almonds, natural peanut butter, and soft/liquid margarines.

Out of all the fats, omega-3 fatty acids have the best reputation because they can help to decrease the risk of blood clots in the arteries. When possible, replace other fats with foods containing omega-3 fatty acids, such as canola and soybean oils, ocean fish, shellfish, soy foods, walnuts, wheat germ, and olive oil.

Trans fats have the worst reputation. Hydrogenation, a chemical treatment, makes fat firmer and may produce effects similar to those of saturated animal fats on the body. For example, stick margarine is hydrogenated and contains more trans fats than liquid or soft margarines. Choose foods that contain no hydrogenated fats or that list them as minor ingredients. In excess, both saturated fats, as those found in butter, and trans fats, as those found in hydrogenated margarine, can cause heart disease. Use them sparingly.

Salmon and other fish with healthy fats, when eaten two times weekly, may help to improve cardiovascular health. While fats are important in a diet, moderation is key with butter, margarine, salad dressings, and so on.

Water

Water is probably the nutrient that is most taken for granted in our society because it is so plentiful and versatile. Water is indispensable to life. Among its many functions, water hydrates the skin, ensures adequate blood volume, moistens the eyes and mouth, and flushes out wastes.

Water also helps maintain metabolism, affecting our energy levels and weight control. Drink at least six to eight (8-ounce) glasses of water per day. (This may include some juices and low-fat milk, but caffeinated beverages do not count.) Weight loss experts concur that diets work best with adequate water consumption. Thirst may even be mistaken for hunger: we may overeat if we are not sufficiently hydrated. Try drinking a glass of water before each meal. If you consume three meals a day, this practice will provide half of the daily recommended intake of water, and you will tend to eat less food. So, drink up!

Here are some additional reasons that we should drink six to eight glasses of water per day:

- Over half of our weight is water.

- Water is the essential component of body fluids, such as digestive juices, blood, urine, lymph, perspiration, mucous, and saliva.

- Cell function and organ function depend on water.

- Water is essential for lubrication.

- Water bathes the joints, helping them to work properly.

- Water moves food through the intestines (and prevents constipation).

- Water helps to regulate body temperature.

AVOID THE HYPE

When beginning a journey, it is important to know your destination. And the road to good health is a journey. Don't be sidetracked or derailed by unsubstantiated dietary claims or "miracle" diets. Deviations from normal recommendations (including low-fat and low-sugar foods; moderate protein; and adequate fruits, vegetables, and whole-grain and dairy products) should be taken cautiously, with advice from medical professionals.

The high-protein, low-carbohydrate diet may not be wise for some people. But most of us would benefit from cutting back on sugar and starches, such as white bread. And consuming more protein, especially in the form of ocean fish (preferably broiled, grilled, or baked), is usually helpful, since these provide heart-healthy omega-3 fatty acids. Diets that are high in beef and pork may provide more protein, but they also contain excess saturated fats and cholesterol, which may harm proper cardiac function.

Weight loss alone does not ensure health. Good health is a multifaceted condition encompassing good diet, physical activity, and appropriate lifestyle habits. Don't jump on the wagon before you know where it's taking you.

VARIETY IN YOUR DIET

The old adage "Variety is the spice of life" applies not only to our surroundings and activities but also to our diet. Nutritionally, there is no one "perfect" food. The body needs over 40 different nutrients a day! Fruits and vegetables are rich in vitamins but low in protein. Dairy products provide abundant calcium but very little iron. Meat and meat alternatives are high in protein but lack important phytochemicals and antioxidants.

The essential nutrients our bodies need are dispersed over a wide range of foods; therefore, a healthy diet depends on variety. Varying your diet is more than choosing food from the different food groups; you also must choose foods that benefit both the body and mind. The following lists are provided by Michael F. Roizen, M.D., as interviewed on *Oprah* some years ago.

BENEFICIAL BRAIN FOODS[2]

- cereal
- watermelon
- apples (unpeeled)
- pumpkins
- berries
- green or black tea
- tomato-based products
- beans
- broccoli
- wild salmon (canned)
- soy

FOODS THAT CAUSE AGING[2]

- white bread
- whole milk
- processed foods
- pastries
- soda
- movie popcorn

AGING ANTIDOTE[2]

- tomatoes

A healthy diet must consist of a variety of foods that benefit both the body and mind. Variety in your diet, along with portion-control and exercise, can help you age well in your 60s and beyond.

———————————— • ● • ————————————

"Eating small portions from the food plate every four hours will keep my energy raging. Health and energy are hot commodities for the 60-plus woman."
—Shirley W. Mitchell's Diary

———————————— • ● • ————————————

QUESTIONS FOR REFLECTION AND APPLICATION

1. Have you left some part of your health up to chance? What choices can you make about your health now?

2. What weaknesses do you have in your diet? How can you improve them?

3. Which types of exercise do you presently incorporate into your daily routine? What can you do to improve your overall fitness?

SEVEN SIMPLE LIFESTYLE SECRETS

1. Don't eat after 8 PM.

2. Drink six to eight (8-ounce) glasses of water a day.

3. Don't consume "empty calories"—foods with no health benefits whatsoever.

4. Exercise regularly.

5. Go easy on the "bad" fats.

6. Get your beauty sleep.

7. Meditate on Scripture.

LONGEVITY PROMISE

"I am the living bread that came down out of heaven; if anyone eats of this bread, he shall live forever."
—John 6:51

EASY, HEALTHY RECIPES

Creamed Spinach

1 package frozen spinach
4 tablespoons low-fat cream cheese
Prepare spinach according to package directions. Stir in cream cheese.

(One cup equals 2 servings of vegetables and 315 mg calcium.)

Easy Chicken and Broccoli Stir-fry

Serves 4

2 boneless, skinless chicken breasts, sliced thinly
2 packages frozen broccoli spears (slightly thawed)
1/2 onion, sliced
1 clove garlic, minced
2–3 tablespoons olive oil
1/4 cup peach preserves
salt and pepper, to taste

In a large wok or skillet, sauté onions and garlic in olive oil. Add chicken; cook until no longer pink. Add broccoli spears and cook for approximately ten minutes, stirring occasionally. Once broccoli is a little tender, remove from heat and add peach preserves. Mix well. Add salt and pepper, to taste. Serve alone as an entrée or over steamed brown rice.

(Each serving equals 1 meat serving and 2 vegetable servings.)

Fruity Yogurt Parfait

Serves 2

1 cup chopped mixed fresh fruit
1 cup low-fat yogurt (choose flavor)
1/2 cup nut and raisin trail mix

Layer fruit, yogurt, and trail mix in two parfait glasses.

(Each serving equals 1 fruit serving and 150 mg calcium.)

Open-Face Bacon, Tomato, and Cheese Sandwich

Serves 1

1 slice whole-wheat bread
1 teaspoon light mayonnaise
2 slices turkey bacon, cut in half
3 slices tomato
1 ounce low-fat cheddar cheese, shredded

Cook turkey bacon according to directions. Toast bread and spread with mayonnaise. Layer cooked bacon and tomato. Top with shredded cheese. Broil in oven until cheese is melted.

(One serving provides 5 grams fiber and 150 mg calcium.)

Light and Healthy PB&J

Serves 1

2 slices whole-wheat bread
2 tablespoons reduced-fat or natural peanut butter
2 tablespoons all-fruit spread (such as Polaner's) or 1 banana, sliced

Spread peanut butter and fruit spread on bread.

(One sandwich provides 5 grams of fiber, as well as essential fatty acids, and phytochemicals. Add a glass of low-fat milk for 300 mg calcium.)

Shirley's Delight
(Fruit Punch)

16 oz. mango nectar
16 oz. papaya nectar
16 oz. guava nectar
1 can passion fruit nectar
3 cups water
1 can (32 ounces) unsweetened crushed pineapple
1 can (16 ounces) mandarin oranges
8 oz. bing cherries
32 oz. ginger ale

The day before you plan to serve the punch, chill punch bowl and ingredients in the refrigerator.

Combine mango, papaya, and guava nectars in a large bowl; stir well. Add passion fruit nectar and water, and then add the crushed pineapple and mandarin oranges. Stir well for five minutes. Add cherries. Refrigerate mixture for 15 to 20 minutes. Remove from refrigerator and slowly pour in ginger ale. Stir for about two minutes. Cover with plastic wrap and chill overnight.

Stir and let sit for three minutes before serving. After ladling the drink into the glasses (being sure to get some of the fruit from the bottom), pour a little of the cherry juice into the glass. The juice will settle on the bottom, giving the beverage a layered look. You may also desire to garnish the sides of the bowl with fresh fruit, such as oranges, lemons, limes, and papaya.

Endnotes

1. Martha Bolton, *Cooking with Hot Flashes: And Other Ways to Make Middle Age Profitable* (Minneapolis, MN: Bethany House, 2004), 73.

2. Michael F. Roizen, M.D., as interviewed on *Oprah* (8 September 2004).

CHAPTER 12

RITES OF PASSAGE

"Change is inevitable—except from a vending machine."
—Robert C. Gallagher

"You will know also that your descendants will be many,
and your offspring as the grass of the earth.
You will come to the grave in full vigor,
like the stacking of grain in its season."
—Job 5:25–26

A sedan pulls up to the sun-dappled woods. An older couple gets out, the wife spry and energetic, the husband grouchy and dark. Norman Thayer (Henry Fonda) wears a country suit and looks uncomfortable in his surroundings. But perhaps he is just uncomfortable with himself. Ethel (Katharine Hepburn) comes prepared with her safari-style outfit and joyful entrance.

Norman's crankiness accompanies them into the cabin. "It's a mess, isn't it?"

"Oh, we'll have it in shape in no time," replies Ethel.

Norman strides over to the window and throws open the curtain. In the fresh light, he rests his gentleman's hat on the rack. His fingers glide over his fishing rods alongside the mirrored hat rack, as if to coax a memory of better days back into them. He stoops over to peer at the pictures under the mirror: one of himself as a champion swimmer, buff and virile; a newspaper clipping about his retirement as a professor; and a photo of a smiling, younger version of himself. He smiles slightly at the thought, then straightens and looks at his reflection in the mirror. His smile freezes and fades into a near grimace. His face is now aged and spotted.

Norman reaches for a fishing cap and sets it on his head. With a faint grunt, he turns away from his reflection.

He is demanding, forgetful, and bored. He scans the newspapers for "help wanted" ads, unwilling to admit that, at age 79, he is through with work. But his work has just begun, and it is much larger than bringing home the bacon. His task now is to make peace with himself—and his family. So begins the movie *On Golden Pond*. The scene may not be altogether unfamiliar for those of us faced with the changes that accompany retirement.

THE AGE OF RETIREMENT

Retirement affects a lot more than our monthly paycheck. And, as with everything else, when it comes to retirement, one size doesn't fit all. It helps to acknowledge both the pros and cons of this season as we prepare for what it has in store.

The Pros of Retirement

The benefits of retirement go beyond getting a senior citizen discount card (though I certainly don't mind receiving 10 percent off my grocery store purchase on Wednesdays and cheap rates at the movie theater).

Deborah loves the flexible schedule and freedom that she has in her 60s. She can dash over to her grandson's classroom at the last minute to volunteer, give her neighbor a lift to the doctor, and still wake up long after the predawn commuters have chugged past her home toward the busy highway.

Freedom is one of the greatest benefits of retirement. It's not all bad to trade in your work ID and be free of the time-card machine after years of driving in rush-hour traffic. Freedom from expectations, from the fear of displacement or irrelevancy, and from having to "produce" allows us to take a deep breath of relief.

With her children grown and gone, Lorinda moved to a warmer climate. Because Perry and Grace had invested wisely, they were able to purchase small homes on opposite sides of the United States so that they could split their time between their children, strengthening their bonds with their kids and grandkids.

Perhaps the greatest gain in the retirement years is the freedom to choose who we will be. Women who live to 65 can expect to see their 80s. That means that the 60s are a golden chance to create a second life, one that's totally different from the first, which may have been defined by others' expectations and demands.

The Cons of Retirement

Granted, there are significant setbacks to retirement. Just as characters have shadow sides, so do the retirement years. In the movie *About Schmidt*, Jack Nicholson faced this demoralizing dilemma when he left his company after many years: he had no reason to wake up, no friends outside work, and no relationship with his wife.

When Mary retired, she enjoyed the reprieve from the work-load just about as long as she would a vacation. After a short while, she missed her circle of work friends and colleagues.

The flip side of having fewer expectations to meet is that, without deadlines, we may feel dead! To go from spending our days meeting people's needs, reading e-mails in an inbox filled with urgent requests, and responding to constant crises that demand our expertise, to finding ourselves without the need to even set the alarm clock, can be demoralizing. The loss of intellectual challenge needn't incapacitate us, however. We just have to find new ways to stretch our minds and exercise our abilities.

One of my friends was the captain of the guards at a penitentiary, and he regularly lunched with important figures in the city. After retirement, no one called him "Captain" anymore, and his "power lunch" meant heating leftovers in the kitchen. His wife said, "He still needs someone to boss around—and I ain't it."

Furthermore, regular paychecks boost our self-esteem, and it is difficult to adjust when we no longer receive them. Social Security and pensions do not quite fulfill our emotional need. Many of us wonder where our affirmation will come from, if not from our day jobs—whether we worked outside the home or saw to the needs of a busy family.

Some women in their 60s are widowed or divorced, and women typically live longer than men. Whether single or married, though, this season can account for a third of our lives. We need a game plan for playing well, as we did in the other two-thirds of our lives. In the first third, we thought about our future, figured out how to get the job we wanted, planned our weddings, and started our families. In the second, we accomplished our goals in our chosen career paths and/or relationships.

Later on, we find that we planned the "moment" of retirement but not the lifestyle. How will we fill our time? What will be meaningful to us and others? Will our lives make a difference?

HELP ON THE HOME FRONT: DEALING WITH MIDLIFE MALADIES

Some believe retirement is overrated—particularly the wives! After eavesdropping at a beauty shop, one woman said, "No one I've talked to likes her husband home all the time."

"Your father is always under my feet," a friend's mother complained. "Every time I turn around, I nearly trip on him. He listens in on every conversation and wants to know what I'm doing every minute of the day. I cannot live this way any longer."

My friend decided it was time for an intervention. She met with her parents and begged them to figure out way to add meaning to their days: volunteer at the library, tutor at a school, take free courses at the local college, participate in separate Bible studies at church, or help in the nursery. Her premise: if you do something life-giving apart from your spouse, you can return home with something to talk about besides how the other person doesn't meet your needs or fulfill your life.

Unfortunately, her efforts failed. Her father, a retiree in his 70s, was content with his life. Her mother had always been miserable in her marriage, yet she saw no reason to change now. It was, after all, her house to run. "He needs to get his own life," she said of her husband. Stubbornness, especially on the part of both spouses, is a lose-lose situation.

We have two options: we can spend our retirement years passively waiting for our spouse to get a life and to leave us alone in ours, or we can develop a plan of action to become the best person we can be. Because, if we change, others will have to change in response to our new moves. In other words, if we get a life, our spouse will be forced to find one, too.

This is one of the delightful tasks we have in the sensational 60s: getting a life. We no longer have to meet others' expectations. "Getting a life" is the perfect salve for "midlife maladies."

Trouble on the Home Front

One of the biggest challenges facing retirees is figuring out how to live under the same roof as a spouse. But there is good news: help is on the way.

Linda said, "I am finally learning how to have a fight. For the first 30 years, we rarely resolved conflict. John traveled with work, and when I felt crazed over something he'd said or done, I asked myself, *Is this worth fighting over?* Since he would be gone the next day, I always decided it didn't matter. Now, we are together every day, and it *does* matter. We have to resolve skirmishes so they don't become wars."

Perhaps we have buried the hatchet before examining it. Here are some pointers to overcoming fights:

- Figure out your own feelings. What bothers you? What is the underlying message you perceive in your spouse's words or actions?

- Invite your husband to speak from his heart. For instance, "How are you feeling about the children leaving? About the rest of your life? About...?"

- Listen to your husband as he shares his feelings. Don't interrupt him or try to figure out your rebuttal.

- Try to rephrase his words to ensure that you're on the same page. Say, for example, "It sounds like you feel _____. Is that right?"

- Listen to the heart. When we get down to the heart of the issue, we find we have a lot in common: hope, fear, longing, insecurities, loss, love.

- Believe the best about your mate, and bring out his best by naming his strengths.

- Don't minimize your own feelings or ignore them altogether. Try saying (not shouting) something along the lines of, "I was hurt when you said...."

- Don't react or overreact to another's overreaction. Escalation never solves conflict, but calmness can defuse a bomb.

- Take a deep breath. If things get hot, get out of the kitchen for a while so that neither of you cooks. Agree to come back in when your tempers have died down. But be sure to do so!

Attention to Tension

In our retirement years, as our attention shifts from our jobs and children to our spouse, we may experience some tension as we find ourselves asking, Who is this person? How do we talk to each other? One woman said, "I was waiting for this time [retirement] so I could meet my husband's eyes, but I don't know what to look for there, and I'm afraid I won't find it when I do look."

Women who are married to overachievers may look forward to having more time to spend with their husbands for intimacy, travel, and hanging out. But the overachieving husband may dread doing anything but working. The opposite danger is that the husband will want to just stop altogether, while his wife is ready to dance all night.

At some point, we must face our unhealthy inability to sit still. But balance is crucial, as well. If we sit too long, we will atrophy, as will our relationships. Finding a new shared hobby can make both the present and the future crackle with excitement.

A couple of city slickers decided to tackle something that neither of them knew anything about. They bought a farm in the country and renovated it. As they worked the land, they got to know new parts of themselves and of each other, thereby discovering a newfound mutual respect.

Be creative in pursuing adventure, whether you're 60 and single or in a middle-aged marriage. Doing something you have never tried before may be just the ticket to a new, life-giving escapade. Create common interests with a friend or spouse, explore new territory, and watch the flame of your love rekindle.

Out of Fury and into Love

Olive was long past the "he loves me, he loves me not" stage of romance. Furious with her husband and through with her marriage, she sat in her den, photo albums on her lap, and began to remove every picture of the man she had grown to despise.

But, as she looked at the snapshots, her breath calmed; her anger subsided. She remembered the man she'd married, the one who'd run through the park carrying her on his shoulders, who'd stayed up all night crafting a piece of furniture, who'd sung outside her window when they were courting…and she fell in love again. A booster shot for midlife marriage is to remember the reasons you first fell in love with each other.

The Boomerang Nest

An empty nest is appealing for many parents who have never had a romantic moment alone at home. But many houses have "revolving-door syndrome": one child leaves, and another returns. Divorced or unemployed adult children will return home while they are trying to get back on their feet again; whole families move in with grandparents while their new home is being built. One senior said, "I'm not to the empty nest stage yet! They keep flying back." It can be both a joy and a headache.

In the "full nest again" stage of parenting, it becomes crucial for us to set emotional, physical, and financial boundaries in order to maintain our identities. How do we help our children without making them dependant on us? How do we keep time for ourselves, for our own dreams and needs, when our children come to us in need? What can we do to help them on their feet again?

Flying Solo

Many seniors find themselves single again, having lost mates to death or divorce. And many are beginning to date. With more freedom from responsibility, and with a sexuality that is lifelong, these seniors will be kicking up their heels on the dance floor. Wedding bells may ring again!

On the other hand, singleness can be scary and dangerous. At 60 and beyond, loneliness may propel us into making bad choices, from dating out of desperation to engaging in dangerous sexual activity. The AIDS Hotline reports:

By 1983, when scientists isolated the human immunodeficiency virus (HIV) as the cause, 1,300 Americans had died—most of them under 40. Thirty years on, though, AIDS is increasingly a disease of older people, who make up the fastest-growing segment of the HIV-positive population. Of the estimated 1.1 million Americans with HIV, some 407,000 are over 50.[1]

According to AARP, one in seven new diagnoses of HIV or AIDS is in a person over 50.[1] It is important to be firm about setting dating guidelines and boundaries. Many women do not give men their home address or telephone number but will meet them at a neutral location agreed upon beforehand. Other women who are disappointed with the local "supply" of available men have turned to the Internet and met potential matches through online Christian dating.

Figuring Out Finances: How Shall We Then Live?

One of the main concerns we face in our 60s is how to finance this season of our lives. Planning financially for retirement is a little like visiting a "fun house" on Halloween: you never know just what horror might pop out at you next. Plan as they may, there are still too many who are taken by surprise by economic downturns and other fiscal fiascos in their later years.

Because the lifespan of the average American is longer than it was in years past, we must look into financing the final third of our lives. Most reports indicate that seniors do not save enough money prior to retirement to maintain their lifestyles. And many people wonder whether they will ever be able to afford to retire at all.

Some are surprised by financial concerns that they hadn't known to worry about. One woman said, "I could retire if I didn't need health insurance. Don't even mention homeowner's insurance and car insurance." Another said, "I didn't know insurance could cancel me. But my homeowner's canceled me after my house was vandalized, the roof was damaged by hail, and the kitchen floor was replaced after it was flooded."

These women are not alone in their dismay. AARP reported that in 2009, 18.7 percent of seniors 65 years and older were living below the poverty line.[2] It is no surprise that in order to stave off retirement worries and other financial concerns, many Americans have ditched their rocking chairs and headed back into the workforce.

Hi Ho, Hi Ho, It's Back to Work We Go

Those who say retirement is overrated are in luck—more than ever before, the 60-plus crowd is now working longer, retiring later, and even heading back to work after retiring in order to provide for their grandkids.

Ed saved his money and retired early. Believing he had what it took to dabble in the stock market, he did—and lost everything. He had to figure out a new way to support himself. Ed is just one of the many who must reinvent themselves after retirement.

To fight against inflation and the fear of future financial problems, Juanita signed on with a temp agency. She sometimes works two jobs at the same time. "It keeps my mind fresh, keeps me learning," she pointed out. It also allows her to put everything she earns into savings, for the day when she and her husband cease to live off of his salary.

WAYS TO LIVE MEANINGFULLY

Another challenge that women face in their 60s is to live meaningfully. This requires engaging our minds, our spirits, our energy, and our longings. We must keep developing all our faculties for work, learning, and play.

Changing Careers

Career reinvention occurs almost daily. While I coped with the loss of my marriage, my friend Carolyn gave me a job in her book distribution company. Meeting new people, calling on the various accounts, and regaining my independence put me on the tarmac for takeoff into a new, fulfilling life. This job gave me the courage to continue with my dream of writing.

This has been true for thousands of others, as well. After years of serving in the military as a doctor, David retired and opened his own practice. His wife, a nurse, had spent many years mentoring women before she began working in tandem with him, helping women sort through the issues no one talks about. This couple is hanging on by a thread, financially, but they have never felt so alive.

"Cocooning," which we discussed in chapter 8, is another increasing trend. More people are choosing to operate a business from home. Retirees enjoy the flexibility of being their own boss, adding to their retirement fund, and increasing business through the Web.

After retiring, many teachers take part-time jobs teaching at a college or move out of state and continue teaching, so as not to forfeit their retirement benefits. Others find that their area of expertise is suited for another industry; for example, a foreign language teacher may begin working for a social service agency or as an interpreter.

Dr. J. I. Packer, author of the book *Knowing God*, spoke of his career in this way: "God has prepared a square hole for a square peg. Packer is my name, and packing is my game. For me, being an author is comparable to a woman giving birth—great pain during delivery, yet great satisfaction afterwards. I can only write because I'm driven to it. And I sweat away. God has laid the task of communication on me."

Dr. Packer's words could have been my own. In my own heart, I felt that God had been preparing me to be His servant, traveling and speaking encouragement to women. And midlife had been the perfect time to pursue that calling.

Continuing Education

One of the greatest benefits of being 60-something is the opportunity to refire our brains and our enthusiasm. Most community colleges offer a senior discount for select courses. There are also online classes, as well as classes offered through community organizations, such as the YMCA and retirement centers.

Dennis and Nora enrolled in a three-year course for leadership training, complete with homework and group accountability meetings. They were both leaders in their previous church and community, but they lacked official training. Plus, they have found that learning together feeds their marriage. Nora has also found that it gives Dennis something to do besides "following [her] around like a puppy."

Volunteering

Imagine what could happen if every sensational-after-60 man and woman volunteered regularly in one of the thousands of places crying out for help. They would change the world, giving others a new lease on life and health.

Uninteresting people are deadly, and people without interests die. Part of the danger of retirement is the temptation to think only of self. On the other hand, when we invest in others, our own health increases and our outlook improves—and our lot in life doesn't look so bad, after all.

Ellen and Charles, both doctors in their 50s, are thrilled as they consider their sixth decade. They can't wait to set up a medical facility in a mission field.

Betsy has run a successful company for years, and she is lining up a dream team to take over so that she may be free to participate in short-term mission trips.

At age 62, Joanne joined the Peace Corps, packed her bags for Africa, and never looked back.

When we invest in something that will outlast our lives, we wake up every day with a reason to get up and go. Volunteering is another way to stretch our minds and continue learning, discovering new things about the people we are serving and how we can better use our skills to help them.

Honing New Skills

The 60s bring another exciting possibility for late bloomers and busy, career-minded people. This is the season to investigate interests we've hardly dared look in the eye up until this point: operating a computer, taking art lessons, learning how to fly-fish.

A 92-year-old woman showed up at my favorite writers' conference, Write-to-Publish, in Wheaton, Illinois. Even in the midst of writing her zillionth novel, she said, "I still have a lot to learn."

Honing our skills on the whetstone of opportunity renews self-worth, reminding us that we are capable and needed and that we can still grow. After all, the sixth decade is a perfect time *"to prepare [ourselves] for works of service, so that the body of Christ may be built up until we all reach unity in the faith"* (Ephesians 4:12–13 NIV).

Never say, "I'll never be able to do that." At age 45, Karen takes ballet, one of her first loves. Her inspiration is the instructor, who, in her 80s, is still limber enough to perform every move she mastered in her youth. "I'll never be old after dancing with her," Karen said.

Exploring the Universe—or Your Own Backyard

Another life-expanding possibility in our newfound freedom is travel. Remember, you don't have to be married to travel. If loneliness and fear keep you at home, join a tour group in which the sponsor makes all the arrangements. This type of tour provides safety, companionship, fun, and a new landscape for our memory banks.

Travel needn't be costly. Commuter trains into cities offer cheap transit into a world of museums, plays, architectural tours, and other local wonders. Public transportation increases our independence and keeps the costs down. Elderhostel, a nonprofit organization, and AARP, offer wondrous educational and traveling adventures.

Whether we drive downtown or across the continent, whether solo or with a group of friends, safety is less of an issue now for women than it was in the past. In-car navigation systems, such as OnStar, and GPS devices make travel safer for women. With these systems, we needn't worry about getting lost, locked out, or left alone in an emergency.

Furthermore, the popularity of cruises continues to rise, and there is usually a group discount. The food, entertainment, and activity schedules are all arranged by someone else, which eases the pressure of planning and increases the pleasure of an exotic trip over exciting waters. Having the details arranged by experts helps to allay the worries of inexperienced travelers.

Whether we travel with a purpose or for leisure, we can enjoy getting away from the "same old, same old" world and moving into a new adventure. This may be just the jolt you need to reconnect your body with your emotions, your heart with your mind.

You may want to challenge your limits, broaden your thinking, or fine-tune your mind-body connection. When I had a chance to go to Russia, I hesitated to leave my family, even though my children were mostly grown. My daughter said, "Of course you're going to Russia. This is a no-brainer. You will never get the chance again." She was right. I did go, and now, looking back, I would not trade the experience for anything.

There are thousands of possibilities to broaden our world and to enlarge our circle of life. If we do not take advantage of these options, we may get tunnel vision and forget that a world even exists.

CARING FOR AGING PARENTS—AND YOURSELF

At 60, we may find ourselves caring for our parents just as our nests are emptying and we are ready to fly. In 2009, the National Alliance for Caregiving reported that an estimated 66 percent of caregivers were women, with one-third of them caring for more than one person.[3] Furthermore, in 2005, the Administration of Aging reported that "many caregivers of older people are themselves growing older. Of those caring for someone aged 65+, the average age is 63 years."[4]

One 60-plus woman said of caring for her 80-plus mother, "The love I have for my mother is very strong, but the thought I don't want to be like this is strong, too. Daughters share their mothers' genes. I see what my mother is going through now, and I will work for the next 20 years to not be like her. She has gone downhill since Dad died, and could not start over apart from that life that she shared with him. His suits still hang in the closet. His wedding ring is still on her finger. Reaching for him every morning, she is upset when she can't find him. The only people she wants around her are her children. Antidepressants have changed her personality."

This thoughtful daughter turned this situation into a double blessing: the gift of caring for her mother with tenderness and grace, and the opportunity to prepare for her own future as she ages.

It is a blessing to serve those who have served us—but our strength grows thin without a support system to help sustain us.

You might consider enrolling your loved one in a local senior day program.[5] Not only is this excellent for the participants' self-esteem and socialization; it also provides a much-needed break for caregivers.

If you are a primary caregiver, do not let the stress take you down! Instead, think about how you will care for yourself. Find a mentor who can help you plan for the future. I work daily to increase my brain power, to build body strength, and to keep growing. It is my mission—and it should be your mission, too.

THAT IT MAY BE WELL WITH YOU

The first of the Ten Commandments with a blessing attached is found in Exodus 20:12: *"Honor your father and your mother, that your days may be prolonged in the land which the LORD your God gives you."* Honoring our parents is key to living long. When we honor our parents, God honors us.

There are blessings in being part of the "sandwich generation" (those who are parenting both their children and their parents). Ruth and Dennis Gibson describe one of the blessings in their book, *The Sandwich Years: When Your Kids Need Friends and Your Parents Need Parenting.*[6] The Gibsons suggest blessing our parents by giving them their memory back: telling them stories of growing up that portray them in their strength and tenderness—stories that make them look good. Not only does this give them new old memories; it helps to restore their self-esteem.

Part of honoring our parents is to listen to them with attentiveness and patience. When we hear the same story repeatedly, it's tempting to say, "You told me that already!" But imagine how foolish they feel when they realize that they've been repeating themselves. How much better is it to give them storytelling rights and to be a good audience, again and again? We don't want to live with regrets.

As with all these rites of passage, we never know when the show will close.

—————————— • ● • ——————————

"The best thing I have learned in the new millennium is that when you suddenly turn 60, your spirit does not age."
—Shirley W. Mitchell's Diary

—————————— • ● • ——————————

QUESTIONS FOR REFLECTION AND APPLICATION

1. If you are retired, how might you use your resources, such as your finances and time, wisely? If you haven't retired yet, how can you start planning for that season in advance?

2. List some of the activities that you would enjoy participating in after retirement. How can you honor God with your free time?

3. What are some obstacles that face caregivers? How might they overcome with those obstacles?

SEVEN SECRETS TO A HEALTHY RITE OF PASSAGE

1. In your 60s, be empowered by your self-confidence, knowledge, experience, and boldness!

2. Mix professionalism with a bit of fun, a dash of kindness, and a spoonful of love. Then your passage into this season of your life will be rewarding.

3. Step into your sixth decade with new freedom, new passion for family and friends, and new interests. This will enable you to look forward to getting out of bed each morning.

4. To reach success, never lose sight of your goals, no matter your age.

5. Embrace your talents.

6. Reach success by building an excellent support group and paying it forward by helping others.

7. Take time to smell the flowers and enjoy sunsets.

LONGEVITY PROMISE

"A gray head is a crown of glory;
it is found in the way of righteousness."
—Proverbs 16:31

Endnotes

1. http://www.aarp.org/health/conditions-treatments/info-05-2011/aids-30-years-later.html.

2. http://www.aarp.org/about-aarp/press-center/info-11-2010/AARPReportOlderAdultsHaveHighestPovertyRate.html.

3. The National Alliance for Caregiving and AARP, "Caregiving in the U.S. 2009," (2009): 14. http://www.caregiving.org/data/Caregiving_in_the_US_2009_full_report.pdf.

4. Administration on Aging, "The National Family Caregiver Support Program Resource Guide," (2005): III-9. http://www.lewin.com/~/media/lewin/site_sections/publications/2479.pdf.

5. For information, contact the National Adult Day Services Organization, www.nadsa.org; the Caregiver Action Network, www.caregiveraction.org; the National Alliance for Caregiving, www.caregiving.org; or the National Council on Aging, www.ncoa.org.

6. Dennis and Ruth Gibson, *The Sandwich Years: When Your Kids Need Friends and Your Parents Need Parenting* (Grand Rapids, MI: Baker Book House, 1991), 75–76.

CHAPTER 13

LOVE, LIBERTY, LONGEVITY

"You get love by participating in it."
—Joan Erikson

*"Strength and dignity are her clothing,
and she smiles at the future."*
—Proverbs 31:25

Love, liberty, and longevity are the three key words of suc-cessful aging. We all crave love and intimacy. Liberty is the birthplace of creativity and happiness. And longevity due to health allows us more time to celebrate life. By introducing role models, sharing godly principles, and teaching new attitudes, this chapter will enhance our aging life with love, liberty, and longevity.

ALL WE NEED IS LOVE

The Beatles had it right all along: Our deepest longing in life is for love—to be loved by someone who will never leave or forsake us. And now, in our 60s, we are in one of several camps: we have tasted a fabulous love with a husband, but it still was not perfect; we have been married, but have never felt that type of love; we have loved and lost; or we are single and longing for a love that will never let us go.

Proverbs 19:22 says, *"What a person desires is unfailing love"* (NIV). At 60-something, if we don't have a love like that in our lives, or if we ache from the disappointment of a love that failed, or if we still yearn for that kind of life…it's good.

The very longing for a love that surpasses anything we can experience on earth is a sign from above. It is a longing for a heavenly love, for a relationship that will never disappoint but will always surprise and be on time. The longing for perfect, all-encompassing love, as well as the disappointment when we do not experience that love in marriage, points to something much greater than earthly love. We desire a love that transcends temporal longings, a love that ultimately leaves us gasping for air and wishing for an upgrade or a newer model.

In his essay *The Weight of Glory*, C. S. Lewis said that of all the beauty and passion we may experience in this world, "They are only the scent of a flower we have not yet found."[1] He compared our longing for love on earth to a child who is happy to make mud pies in the slums because he cannot imagine a holiday at the sea.

What we find in earthly love is not the infallible, never-leave-me kind of love we seek. The love we find on earth is made of shadows, of faint whiffs of a greater love—a love that surpasses our imagination.

Our longings were never intended to be satisfied by our earthly relationships. When the best that this world has to offer does not fit the bill, we are finally in a place to find true love.

Perhaps you are in a place of longing at this time. After 60 years of living, there is not a man in sight to love you. Or perhaps the love of your life turned out to be less than you expected. Your need for intimacy has not been fulfilled.

Look no further. There is a Savior who will love you without end, who is building a mansion for you in heaven, and who cannot wait to lavish you with love and attention and gifts. His name is Jesus. If you have never had a man give his life for you, look no further! Jesus already has—He came; He lived; He died that you might have life, and have it to the fullest. (See John 10:10.)

If you have never experienced a love that satisfies your deep-est longings, take a moment now to invite Jesus to live in the very midst of those desires. If you are tired of making mud pies, let this Lover take you on an eternal holiday by the sea! You can pray a prayer like this:

Jesus, I believe that You came to save me and to love me.
I know I don't deserve that love; I can't possibly earn it.
I know that I have sinned and that my sins separate me
from You. Please forgive me. Please come and live in my
heart. Please come and love me.

And He will. *"But as many as received Him, to them He gave the right to become children of God, even to those who believe in His name"* (John 1:12). *"How great a love the Father has bestowed upon us, that we should be called children of God; and such we are"* (1 John 3:1). *"And hope does not disappoint, because the love of God has been poured out within our hearts through the Holy Spirit who was given to us"* (Romans 5:5).

Welcome to the family!

FINDING FULFILLMENT IN MARRIAGE

How do we build honest and legitimate intimacy in our mar-riages and other relationships? How do we live out this love on earth, in human relationships? Ross Campbell's surprising book, *How to Really Love Your Child*, points out three simple means of communicating love that are essential if we are to believe and receive love. These three means are (1) eye contact, (2) focused attention, and (3) touch. These work in every relationship, and they are especially important in marriage. Who doesn't want to feel like the center of attention? Anytime we seek the heart of another, we build intimacy.

Sex at 60

To feel feminine at 60 is priceless. We can experience deeper emotions during sex as we move beyond hormones to harmony. Those who are married later in life move from loneliness to the physical contact of skin against skin; from being a single to the joining of bodies and souls through eye-to-eye contact. From infancy, we crave touch, warmth, and togetherness. These desires are programmed into each of us as part of our software.

The splendor of a sexual relationship between a husband and wife is the climax of joy. The closeness, the fragrance of the lover, the combining of souls, and the intimacy are pure ecstasy. Sex inside marriage is a gift from God. And this gift does not cease at 60.

The problem with some women in their 60s is that they lose their self-esteem due to their waistlines. They compare themselves with younger women and feel that they fall short of the ideal image. All of this gets into their psyches, causing them to feel less feminine. Thus, they pull away from their husbands; they don't want to be seen without clothes on. They would do well to remember the words of a doctor at a women's conference: "Your man doesn't care what your body looks like—some wrinkles or extra pounds—as long as it's naked!"

Many women have a hard time believing this, however, and their withdrawal can create a sexual chasm between herself and her husband—a divide that becomes harder and harder to cross. Sometimes, physical problems like erectile dysfunction, the effects of blood pressure medicine, and other issues make sex awkward. Add to this the natural effects of aging, when the hormones aren't raging like they were in our youth, and the sexual picture can seem bleak.

But there is life after 60! *Time* magazine ran an article titled "The Kids Are Gone. The House Is Empty. You Know the Moves. What Better Time to Prove That You're…Still Sexy after 60." Frederic Golden wrote in a different article, "Without fear of unwanted pregnancy—worries about kids barging into the bedroom—older couples have much less reason to be uptight about sex. They are also much more likely to be adept at pleasing each other, knowing where and how to arouse."[2] They experience what anthropologist Margaret Mead called "Post-Menopausal Zest."

Sex isn't only about the body; it's a product of the head and the heart. It isn't solely about intercourse; it is an approach to a relationship, a way of building an intimacy that involves loving touch and focused attention and care for the other person. The actual consummation is only a part of the big picture. After 60, sex requires more caring and understanding and motivation, which means that it becomes an increasingly selfless act—a demonstration of love, as well as passion.

When Love Disappoints

Marriage isn't all it's cracked up to be, according to many women's experiences. They are lonely in their marriages. They feel that their deep longings have been overlooked. They feel withered instead of fulfilled, emotionally abandoned rather than embraced. According to a survey sponsored by K-Y Brand, 77 percent of women crave more romance in their marriage, and 25 percent do not remember their last date with their husbands.[3] How do we meet our needs for intimacy? How do we meet our needs for love in a way that is legitimate and pure?

One woman said, "My friends have saved me there." She cultivates friends in all age groups, so that they are like a "bank I can withdraw from." These women support each other, loan their shoulder to cry on, and laugh together.

Your spouse was never intended to be your sole emotional and psychological support. We were created for many relationships of varying degrees of closeness, and our female friends can meet many of those needs. This allows us to feel fulfilled in our souls and energized for daily life, even if our marriage is less than perfect.

Therefore, do not burden your husband trying to find complete fulfillment in him. God made women special. He created them to be sensitive, beautiful creatures, who find complete fulfillment in Him. This is why a 60-year-old woman can live a complete, balanced life, even without a partner or a husband. When her fulfillment is found in Christ alone, a woman is able to stand firm, whether single, married, divorced, or widowed. She is able to live with passion because each day given to her on this earth is complete in Christ.

SEXY AND SINGLE

If you are single, or if you find yourself in an unfulfilling marriage when it comes to intimacy, let your loneliness teach you about yourself. Do not allow loneliness to cause you to settle for bad relationships, or you may end up choosing the wrong mate. Instead, learn about yourself. Self-knowledge helps us to understand what we desire in a date or a mate.[4]

Turn Desires into Action

If you are single, invest your unfulfilled desires into some-thing you are passionate about, something that gives you an adrenaline rush, a feeling of self-worth. Channel your desires into legitimate, meaningful, healthy activities. No whining! No self-pity! Don't allow the lack of a husband to make you feel like any less of a woman. Many women who have broken off relation-ships discover a newfound freedom and sense of independence that allows them to find who they really are, at which point they really don't want another relationship like marriage.

In *New Passages*, Gail Sheehy writes,

While divorce is always painful, it is seen in retrospect as a springboard by many of the women....The forced assertion of self, plus the educational pursuits so many have resumed, open up whole new range of possibilities for progress as women grow older....Having earned their self-confidence through crisis and turmoil, they guard it fiercely. A recent study of several hundred "typical" white middle-class American women front-runners of the baby boom generation, and their slightly older coun-terparts, confirmed that divorce spurs a woman's psy-chological growth: Suddenly single—whether by choice or default—most felt unburdened for the first time in their lives. And they weren't risking remarriage if it meant being restricted. They were out to discover who they were.[5]

The best way to use your time in your sexy, single 60s is to become the women you were meant to be. You can feel good, lovely, feminine, and needed, regardless of your marital status. Interestingly enough, this is appealing to many men, who find it alluring when a woman is content in her own skin and feels good about herself, with or without a man. Joan Erikson said, "Having a husband can be such an alibi for a woman; in the end she never lives her own life…a full life needs to be about self-cultivation."[6]

In our sixth decade, we see that we have lived much of our lives meeting other people's needs and agendas—our spouse, our boss, our parents, our kids. Now we get to figure out who we are without worrying as much about other people's needs. For those of us who have deferred our dreams and delayed living fully, now is the time to seize the moment, seize the day, and seize the decade.

This doesn't mean we should live selfishly for the rest of our days, becoming narcissistic and focusing solely on our own wants and needs, never again to lift a finger for another person. On the contrary, as we begin to find fulfillment in this decade, as we begin to embrace our gifts, dreams, and needs, we are better equipped to love other people—even when those we love don't quite measure up.

Having Our Needs Met

Our need for intimacy and enjoyment can be met in millions of ways: going to dinner with friends, watching a movie, going on a cruise, joining a singles' group, and so forth. We may be single and 60, but that doesn't mean we have to be alone.

When your self-esteem takes a nosedive, listen up! Some of you have gone your entire life not knowing how wonderful you are. Now is the time to find out! You are sensational, not because of how you look or your relationship status or your career, but because God created you, adores you, and dances over you in delight.[7] (See Zephaniah 3:17.)

When we bring our needs to God, He will always lead us toward life. Jesus said, "*I am the bread of life; he who comes to*

Me shall not hunger, and he who believes in Me shall never thirst" (John 6:35). Jesus Christ sustains our lives and satisfies our deepest desires. His "heavenly bread" never runs out. *"Taste and see that the* LORD *is good"* (Psalm 34:8).

LIBERTY IS A MIND-SET

Liberty begins in our minds and hearts. In the Claymation movie *Chicken Run*, Ginger is a plucky hen who constantly schemes to set free the fellow prisoners in her coop. She is thwarted at every turn, not only by the vigilant farmer, but also by the hens themselves. She says in her brisk British accent, "The fences aren't just 'round the farm. They're up here, in your heads." One of her doom-and-gloom cohorts says, "Face the facts, Ducks: the chances of us getting out of here are a million to one." In response, Ginger squares her face and steels her eyes as she replies, "Then there's still a chance."

The chances of us finding life in our 60s are far better than those of the hens; that is, if we choose to dismantle the fences that the world and we ourselves have set up in our minds. When we tear down the self-imposed limitations on our hearts and minds, as Ginger did, we free ourselves to enjoy life in our 60s and beyond.

Dr. Ken Dychtwald said that women generally have more liberty after 60, unless they are the caretaker of grandchildren, aging parents, or a husband. But even a woman serving as caretaker can enjoy freedom if she lives with liberty as a state of mind. We can choose to serve with joy, as though we were serving Christ Himself. (See Matthew 25:40; Colossians 3:17, 23.) We can choose to find freedom in the beauty of a smile or a sunset, even though we may be locked in the role of caregiver.

Finding Liberty in Change

Liberty may look like changing careers rather than retiring. Let's face it: if we retire at age 62 or 65, we may have 30 years of life left. With what activities are we going to fill our time?

Many women have never had the freedom of choice until reaching their 60s. They move from being supported by their father to caring for a husband and children. The 60s may be the first time many women enjoy the freedom to choose how to spend their time. And we *do* have a choice! We can fill our days pursuing our dreams, passions, and adventures. We can go back to school or learn a new trade. One woman I knew took welding classes at a trade school near her home.

It's time to kick up our heels! A gentleman whom I dated, whose "real" age was 60, was a professional ballroom dancer, and the two of us enjoyed dancing together. One night, we were seated at a table with four other couples. I remember watching one of the women—a beautiful lady dressed to the nines—who sparkled as the spinning lights of the disco ball reflected off of her jewels as she danced. When she sat back down at the table, she put her nasal oxygen cannula back on. A few minutes later, when it was time to dance again, she abandoned her tank and spun around the ballroom, dancing and dancing.

Dance, ladies! As Gail Sheehy says, "Women and men now in their 60s have reached the stage where maximum freedom still coexists with a minimum of physical limitations."[8] Find liberty in the new opportunities that emerge in your 60s.

The longer you live, the more time you have to pursue your dreams. Keep in mind that this usually involves risk. My friend Gay Martin longed to write, but to her, branching out was like climbing out on a very thin limb. Her husband wisely said, "I think you better follow your bliss." In spite of the risk of failure and loss of income, she decided to write. And it's a good thing she did. Her books have touched many people. Among them are *Alabama off the Beaten Path* and *Louisiana off the Beaten Path*.

Taking risks makes our adrenaline flow. And endorphins make us feel buoyant and ready to rock and roll...or at least jog a bit. Women who endure loss, who feel like life has passed them by, or who feel that they don't look as good as they wish may become whiny, needy, depressed, or cranky people who repel others—including their husbands and children. Proverbs 21:19 says, *"It is better to live in a desert land, than with a contentious and vexing woman."*

Do not wait around for life to show up on your doorstep with an embossed invitation. Your passage to 60 *is* the invitation!

LONGEVITY: MORE THAN LIVING LONGER

Living long and living well starts with taking care of ourselves. I cannot overemphasize the importance of exercise and diet or their impact on mind, body, soul, and spirit. Whatever suits you, whatever you have to do, just do it! Keep moving. The better we care for our bodies, the longer they will last, and the less they will depreciate with age. Do not close this book without making a body plan. How you will care for your body daily so that it is equipped to work hard for you the rest of your life?

Exercise in order to build muscle, strengthen your heart, and increase endurance. Dr. Bortz, author of *Dare to Be 100*, said to me several years ago, "If you don't lift weights, you won't be able to lift your grandchildren." I raced straight to the gym! Who we are has less to do with ourselves and far more to do with how we impact others, such as our grandchildren.

Embrace life. Doing things you love to do will help you live longer. Love what you do and hang out with people you love. Try making a list right now of the activities you love and your favorite ways to serve. Then, start doing them! Spend time with those you love. You will live longer when you get outside of yourself and into other people's lives and activities.

When we embrace a lifestyle of love and liberty, longevity is guaranteed. It may not necessarily be in terms of the number of years we live, but it will certainly compute to a high quality of life and to lasting effects on the lives of those around us. As we love others out of the fullness of God's love, and as we begin to walk in the freedom that comes from being loved without restraint by the Creator, the joy in our lives will spill over onto everyone we meet. When we trust God to meet our deepest needs and to help us live out our dreams and calling, lives will be changed—starting with our own!

───── • ● • ─────

"If you fill life with the love, laughter, and the liberty of Jesus, it will be long and happy."
—Shirley W. Mitchell's Diary

───── • ● • ─────

QUESTIONS FOR REFLECTION AND APPLICATION

1. If you are married, consider your love life. Is it as sensational as it could be? If you are single, are you engaging with family and friends enough to keep your human "love tank" full?

2. Second Corinthians 3:17 says, *"Where the Spirit of the Lord is, there is liberty."* Is the Holy Spirit present in your life?

3. Discuss ways in which you can live longer and better. How will you implement these strategies?

SEVEN SIMPLE SECRETS FOR SUCCESSFUL AGING

1. Set your mind at the perfect age and never get any older.

2. Make your journey beyond youth the prime time of your life.

3. Find your fulfillment in Christ before you look to your relationships.

4. Positive attitudes will empower you to be ageless.

5. Knowing God will propel you into everlasting life.

6. What's important is not the years in your life but the life in your years.

7. "Don't waste a day. You don't get the opportunity to go back and repeat life." —Patsy Riley, former First Lady of Alabama

LONGEVITY PROMISE

"Let him who means to love life and see good days refrain his tongue from evil and his lips from speaking guile....Do good...seek peace and pursue it."
—1 Peter 3:10–11

Endnotes

1. C. S. Lewis, *The Weight of Glory and Other Addresses* (Revised and Expanded Edition) (New York: MacMillan Publishing Co., 1980), 6.

2. Frederic Golden, "Still Sexy after 60," *Time* magazine (19 January 2004): 109.

3. Leslie Goldman, "Married Women Crave More Romantic Time with Partners," *Chicago Tribune* (29 September 2004): Sec. 8, 1, 7.

4. Web sites such as eHarmony (www.eharmony.com) offer an interesting possibility for Christian singles meeting one another. This particular site offers a "self-knowledge" test for participants.

5. Sheehy, *New Passages*, 337.

6. Joan Anderson, *A Walk on the Beach: Tales of Women from an Unconventional Woman* (New York: Random House, 2004), 104.

7. For inspiration, listen to the song "I Hope You Dance" by Leeann Womack.

8. Sheehy, *New Passages*, 352.

CHAPTER 14

TURN YOUR 60s INTO A CELEBRATION

"Each day comes bearing its own gifts. Untie the ribbons."
—Ruth Ann Schabacker

"I know that there is nothing better for men than to be happy and do good while they live. That everyone may eat and drink, and find satisfaction in all his toil—this is the gift of God."
—Ecclesiastes 3:12–13 (NIV)

My personality loves to celebrate life. This trait must be programmed into my DNA. Maybe it is, in more ways than one! Christ said, *"I came that they might have life, and might have it abundantly"* (John 10:10).

I celebrated life in my childhood, teens, 20s, 30s, 40s, 50s, and 60s. Every decade has been a jubilee. When I turned 60, beginning the high tide of the Age Wave, I planned to escalate to the grand finale of my life by soaring to new heights of excellence.

I love grand finales. Orchestras and musical companies perform their greatest piece during the grand finale. At every Fourth of July celebration, the best fireworks are saved for the grand finale. Jack London said, "I would rather that my spark would burn out in a brilliant blaze than by dry rot. I would rather be a superb meteor, every atom of me in magnificent glow, than a sleepy and permanent planet. The proper function of man is to live, not exist."

At this point in our lives, life has been building for 60 years, and it is time for our grand finale, which may last 30 years!

One part of our grand finale should be the greatest friendships we've ever known. I have made many wonderful friends along the path of life. Jane and I met ten years ago, and today we are the best of friends. We have enjoyed many joyful experiences along the way. Jane is a lovely lady, nearly six feet tall, very slim, beautiful, and elegant. A spirit of warmth, compassion, hospitality, and joy radiates from her. Ever since the day we met, we have not stopped celebrating. Together we have met writing deadlines, traveled, interviewed, and prayed. We cheer for each other. We support one another as our network grows and our circle of life expands. I feel 20 years younger when I am with Jane.

Celebrating life is a continual feast with my family, as well. With three children and seven grandchildren, in addition to their husbands and wives, there is always a birthday, anniversary, holiday, or other special occasion to celebrate. I will share about a couple of these family celebrations with you.

At age 64, I had a new grandbaby—and we have always celebrated life as it happens to us in my family. It was no exception when baby Lawrence was born to my youngest son, Jay, and his wife, LaWanda. LaWanda created the most beautiful christening gown. We went to Jay's church, and our entire family squished into a pew together. After the service, we rented a room in a restaurant and celebrated with a big dinner, and then, in the afternoon, the party spilled over into the proud parents' home.

One Thanksgiving, three of my granddaughters—Michelle, Monica, and Melissa—flew from Cincinnati, Ohio, to come visit me. Their mother, Karen, was to meet them at my home, driving directly from work in Cincinnati.

As we awaited Karen's arrival, my granddaughters and I hung out and munched on goodies in the kitchen. Then, the phone rang. I picked it up, and on other end of the line, I heard Karen say, "Mom, I'm okay, but you need to come to Sardis and pick me up. I was in a wreck."

My heart was palpitating as I arrived on the scene. In the dark, I observed police cars with swirling lights, a fire truck, and Karen's wrecked Volvo. The Volvo Company advertises the safety of the steel cage inside the car. Fortunately, it worked; the impact of the collision had completely destroyed the hood up to the steel cage, but Karen was not hurt.

On the next day, Thanksgiving, our family gathered for a feast at the home of my son David and his wife, Angela. They have three children—Stephanie, Sarah, and Jackson. Also in attendance were my youngest son, Jay; his wife, LaWanda; and baby Lawrence. Before we indulged in the delicious feast, we stood around the table, and David asked each of us to share one thing we were thankful for.

My oldest granddaughter, Michelle, said, "I'm thankful that my mother is here today and that God protected her." Each person, from the youngest to the oldest, expressed one thing for which he or she was thankful. We concluded by holding hands while David prayed our Thanksgiving prayer.

What a privilege it is to gather around the banquet table on Thanksgiving and to give thanks to our Creator—especially when the story could have turned out so much differently. As a grandmother, I have found that Thanksgiving is an excellent metaphor for the second half of my life. Robert Burns once said, "Enjoy the last of life for which the first was made."

This is the time for a celebration! The 60s are superb, and we want the world to know it!

In case some of you are still questioning, here are some reminders. We are:

Sizzling, Not Fizzling

Is it possible to be sizzling after 60, instead of fizzling? There is one woman, in particular, who comes to mind when I hear of the word "sizzling"—Barbara Walters.

Through the years, I have been an avid fan of Barbara Walters and had viewed almost all of her clips that were aired on TV. In her final season on 20/20, a snapshot showed her interviewing U.S. presidents and first ladies, world leaders, and criminals.

After watching her mature with elegant grace over that quarter-century, I was encouraged to see that, even in her 60s, she was not retiring but refiring. She still had the flexibility to create her own television specials. And her brainchild, the very popular ABC morning show *The View*, is still invigorated by her frequent visits. She took a risk when she created the *Barbara Walters Show*. Not everyone thought it would succeed.

But she would not, and will not, fizzle out. This woman is still sizzling.

Savvy, Not Sad

Is it possible to be savvy, not sad, at 60? Absolutely! My time on the panel of judges for the 2004 American Classic Woman of the Year Pageant (formerly called the Ms. Senior Alabama Pageant) proved this to be true. I enjoyed serving alongside Ms. Senior Calhoun County 2001 Jean Johnson, first runner-up for

Ms. Senior Alabama, and Mr. Bobby Rice, a retired teacher and vice president of AARP of Marshall County, Alabama. "Aging with Grace" was an appropriate theme for the pageant.

The American Classic Woman of the Year Pageant recognizes women who face life's ups and downs with inner strength, humor, and resilience. The pageant encourages women over 60 to continue to grow and achieve. By providing a public forum for the women to present their past, present, and future ambitions, the pageant gives them an opportunity to encourage women of all ages. The pageant celebrates the achievements, dedication, beauty, and spirit of the classic woman. It acknowledges the determination and passion of the classic senior woman as she sets a positive example for other women.

The eight contestants were judged on their individual interviews, talent, and poise. And all of them were winners. They all represented the new "old" by aging outside of the box with power, style, and vitality.

Ms. Mary B. Young was crowned Ms. Alabama Classic Woman in 2004. She shared her philosophy of life: "Live, love, and laugh. Look forward to the future with confidence. When you are faced with decisions, make those decisions as wisely as possible, and then go on. Be happy and enjoy what is beautiful. Dance like nobody's watching and love like it's never gonna hurt."

The participants in this pageant were savvy, not sad!

A WOW, Not a "Woe Is Me" Woman

Is it possible to be a WOW (wonderful older woman) rather than crying "Woe is me" as we age? Wonderful older women exemplify strength, positive attitudes, alert minds, attractive appearances, passion, enthusiasm, and vigor.

Instead of crying "Woe is me," the WOW focuses on...

• the possibilities of aging, not the problems.

• the opportunities of aging, not "old lady syndrome."

• reinventing herself, not deteriorating.

• God's calling, not empty, worldly success.

ARE YOU A WOW?

My favorite WOW, my role model, is Elizabeth Dole. At a prayer breakfast, she said, "Life is not just a few years to spend on self-indulgence and career advancement. It is a privilege, a responsibility, a stewardship to be lived according to a much higher calling—God's calling. In a world where so little seems permanent, we draw from eternal truths, expressed in customs handed on like fine family silver from one generation to the next."

Mrs. Dole's record has been largely influenced by her beliefs. She has a Harvard Law degree and was secretary of transportation during the Reagan administration, secretary of labor during the George H. W. Bush administration, president of the American Red Cross, candidate for president of the United States, and a retired senator from her home state of North Carolina. Now in her mid-70s, she still attends various award dinners and charity functions in Washington, D.C.

Like Elizabeth Dole, you can be extraordinary. You are the only person God made with your own uniqueness. Diderot said, "Only passions, great passions, can elevate the soul to great things." And you are a WOW—you have what it takes!

Lace over Steel, Not Sackcloth over Ashes

Is it possible to cast off the sackcloth and ashes in favor of lace over steel? Yes! Sixty-plus women have a feminine side of lace that covers their strength of steel. Of course, there is a place for grief in aging, but the Bible says that the Lord will *"grant those who mourn in Zion, giving them a garland instead of ashes, the oil of gladness instead of mourning, the mantle of praise instead of a spirit of fainting"* (Isaiah 61:3).

Sixty Is the New Thirty

Is it possible to redefine aging—to become the "new old"? Is 60 today what the age of 30 used to be? Yes! Model and actress Lauren Hutton's face smiled from the cover of the 2003 November/December issue of *AARP Magazine*. The headlines read, "Sixty Is the New Thirty." Lauren rejuvenated her modeling career at the age of 44. This adventurous woman has become an icon for older women, even as she approaches her seventh decade. Hutton believes there is beauty in all ages and sizes.

When you make your life a celebration, you can help redefine aging, so that 60 is truly the new 30.

IS THERE A DOCTOR IN THE HOUSE?

Family, friends, and coworkers gathered in a room filled with personal photos and beautiful flowers to celebrate my sister, Debra Goodwin. What was the occasion? After many years of study and hard work, she had reached her goal—she was now *Dr.* Debra Goodwin.

Debra and I grew up on a farm, surrounded by love, faith, family, and hard work in the cotton fields. Being an A-1 personality—a shaker and a mover—Debra set lofty goals for herself, and she funded her education through student loans. Now a professor at Jacksonville State University, where she has taught for 25-plus years, she has positively influenced thousands of students.

As we celebrated with food, fun, and frolic at this lively event, my grandchildren got to partake in her joy of setting a goal, focusing, working hard, and never giving up. They will remember her victory when they encounter challenges in life. Dr. Debra is an inspiration to the young, as well as to the aging.

Our mother, 84 at the time, wore a beautiful pink suit and white pearls for the occasion. Debra and I had treated her to lunch and a shopping trip to purchase the outfit. What fun! Mom hid these precious moments away in her heart, to pull up in her memory whenever she chooses.

My older children told stories about their aunt Debra. They talked about how, when they were younger, they would always beg to have Debra as their babysitter. I can understand why! I would instruct her to put the children to bed at 8:00 PM, but Debra did not like putting the children to bed, because she felt lonely in the quiet house; so, she would play with them until I returned. When I came home and opened the front door, the children would jump in bed and pretend to be asleep.

Dr. Debra is truly "lace over steel"! She helps me to remember that life is short, fragile, and uncertain; and so, at 60-plus, we must embrace the importance of celebrating life! We cannot let life pass us by. Create a celebration, whatever the event. We are not guaranteed a tomorrow. We have to celebrate today. If it's Monday, toast to a new beginning! If it's the first day of fall, jump in the leaves! If it snows today, make snow angels, have a snowball fight, or build a snow fort. If it's hot outside, wash the car the old-fashioned way (with a hose, a sponge, and a water fight). Simply being alive is cause for celebration!

THE GETAWAY GIRLS

Is there anything better than snagging your girlfriends away and having a ball? For our girls' night out, my friends and I—a redhead, a blonde, and two brunettes—chose to dine at a lovely restaurant. Two of us were dressed in white, two in evening black. When we paraded into the lobby, we made quite a stir.

If you don't feel like playing dress up, you can have a pajama party in your home and invite your best buddies. Or, choose a destination, in the United States or abroad, call your friends, and have a party there! Take a steamboat down the Mississippi River or a raft through the Grand Canyon. Many resorts and hotels offer special weekend packages for a "girls' getaway," including everything from spa treatments to movies and pop-corn. You could also plan a weekend in the woods or at a dude ranch. Whatever you choose—a night on the town or a weekend away—grab your best girlfriends and make it a life occasion.

Let's celebrate. Sixty is sensational!

———————— • ● • ————————

"At 60-plus, we have a smorgasbord
of blessings to celebrate!"
—Shirley W. Mitchell's Diary

———————— • ● • ————————

QUESTIONS FOR REFLECTION AND APPLICATION

1. You may be 60, but you are still you! How are you going to look cool, love yourself, and live it up?

2. Share some of your celebration stories with others.

3. If you received a second chance at life after a near-death experience, how would you celebrate?

SEVEN SECRETS TO CELEBRATING

1. Jump for joy! Make life a celebration!

2. Food, frolic, and fun turn can turn the gray skies into sunshine in the soul.

3. Age "sunny-side up." A smile is a great face-lift.

4. Ace the race of life!

5. Older women with zeal and passion have a continual celebration.

6. Celebrate the youngsters! They allow us to live on after death.

7. Celebrate the gift of years.

LONGEVITY PROMISE

"A joyful heart is good medicine."
—Proverbs 17:22 (NIV)

Endnote

1. Jenny Joseph, "Warning," *Selected Poems* (Chester Springs, PA: Bloodaxe Books, 1992).

CHAPTER 15

MAKE YOUR LIFE A MICHELANGELO

"My trade and my art is living."
—Montaigne

"However many years a man may live,
let him enjoy them all."
—Ecclesiastes 11:8 (NIV)

Sculptor, artist, architect, and poet Michelangelo was born in Florence, Italy, in 1475. He has been called the genius of the Renaissance—the greatest artist ever. Some of his first masterpieces were sculptures, which eventually became his preferred artistic medium. Experts believe that Michelangelo's favorite work was the *Pietà* because it was the only sculpture on which he put his signature. The marble statue is of the Virgin Mary cradling Jesus' body after His crucifixion.

THE PASSION OF THE PIETÀ

Michelangelo carved the *Pietà* in Rome between 1497 and 1500. He was 25 when he finished the legendary piece. A master craftsman, he had the genius to make the *Pietà* an emotional, living piece that is still popular half a millennium later. Viewers of the *Pietà* can see the motherly love of Mary and her deep grief at Jesus' death. It portrays a bond between a mother and child that is extremely strong.

While visiting Rome years ago, I was so moved with emotion by the *Pietà* that I purchased a small marble replica of it from a street vendor. Today, this replica fills a prominent place in my lighted trophy case. This sculpture especially stirs my deep emotions for my two sons, David and Jay.

The love we have for our children and grandchildren grows deeper with age. We have memories of their births, birthdays, childhood, growing pains, successes, failures, celebrations, and milestones deep inside our hearts.

Through our lives, we experience love, intimacy, and pain. These same emotions erupted within my heart as I viewed the sculpture *Pietà*, nearly five centuries after Michelangelo released it from the marble. His work packs a mighty emotional punch! After the *Pietà*, Michelangelo began carving the monumental *David*, perhaps his most well-known piece, portraying great physical and spiritual strength—a sense of grandeur and power.

Our 60 or more years of life are a testimony to our physical and spiritual strength, our sense of grandeur and power. And yet, it is not the years alone that count. Montaigne wrote, "Wherever your life ends, it is all there. The advantage of living is not measured by length, but by use; some men have lived long, and lived little; attend to it while you are in it. It lies in your will, not in the number of years, for you to have lived enough."

Will your legacy outlive you as you leave your chisel marks in the marble of time? What element of your life will live on after you?

THE SISTINE CHAPEL

What a privilege it was to view the Sistine Chapel in the Vatican City. It was so spectacular that it etched a vivid picture in my memory.

In 1508, Pope Julius II summoned Michelangelo to Rome to paint the Sistine Chapel. This titanic task, painting 340 magnificent Bible figures and scenes on a curved surface of about 10,000 square feet, took 20 months—and made him famous. One commentator wrote, "It is astounding that an artist who disliked painting as much as Michelangelo should have achieved universal glory in that art."[1] These stunning frescoes that cover the Sistine Chapel are a product of Michelangelo's awesome talent, focus, and work ethic.

In his book *We Live Too Short and Die Too Long*, Dr. Walter M. Bortz II writes, "It is my best estimate that our biogenetic maximum life span is 120 years—approximately one million hours."[2] Life after 60 has its own titanic tasks. Let's follow Michelangelo's example as we discover how to use our own talents, focus, and work ethic to live out a full life of 120 years—or however many years God gives to us—with health, vitality, and passion.

"TO THE GLORY OF GOD": A LEGACY OF FAITH

Michelangelo, artist, sculptor, architect, and poet—the genius of the Renaissance—"denied that he had any formal training in the arts, preferring to imply that his genius was unique and God-given, owing nothing to any mortal teacher."[3]

At his death on February 18, 1564, at 88 years of age, Michelangelo left a legacy of faith. It is said of him that "the object of painting was to represent the soul. What interested him in the men he painted was their share of the eternal."[4] His life, his being, his work, his passion, and his focus all centered on his faith in God. In March 1555, he wrote in a sonnet, "Make me hate all that the world values, and all its beauties that I honour and revere, so that before death I may lay hold of life eternal."

Though Michelangelo painted the Sistine Chapel under duress on his back, and though the task was fraught with difficulty, the finished product is still considered one of the greatest masterpieces in history[5], even more than five centuries after Michelangelo's death.

Just as the circumstances of Michelangelo's work imbued his art with passion, so the pain and difficulties of our lives can contribute passion to our life's masterpiece. We alone choose how we will respond to the situations we encounter. We have all the necessary tools for a work of genius: the canvas (our life), the gifts, the time, the energy. At 60, we may have 30 more years to create a masterwork!

What will your life's colors be? Will the effects of your life choices extend beyond your last breath, the last stroke of your brush, the last etch on your chisel? Who will benefit from your canvas of contributions to the world? What are those contributions?

Paint your picture of aging with gusto like Michelangelo's. Faith is the paint that will make your aging picture glow with light and exciting color.

• ● •

"Making older life a 'Michelangelo masterpiece' will get me ready for heaven!"
—Shirley W. Mitchell's Diary

• ● •

QUESTIONS FOR REFLECTION AND APPLICATION

1. Has reading about Michelangelo's life inspired you? How?
2. Do you believe your uniqueness is God-given?
3. How will you paint your picture of aging?

SEVEN SIMPLE SECRETS TO "MICHELANGELO" LIVING

1. Break out of routine; it can be the road to failure.
2. Think of doing the opposite of the norm; find another angle.
3. Brainstorm ideas.
4. Adapt the concepts of others.
5. Go to extremes.
6. Imagine in terms of exaggeration.
7. Do the unusual.
8. (A fun bonus): Do the unexpected.

LONGEVITY PROMISE

"Now faith is the assurance of things hoped for, the conviction of things not seen."
—Hebrews 11:1

Endnotes

1. Gilles Nerét, *Michelangelo* (Köln, Germany: Taschen GmbH, 2001, reprinted by Barnes & Noble, Inc., 2001), 23.

2. Walter M. Bortz, *We Live Too Short and Die Too Long* (New York: Bantam Books, 1991), 10.

3. Jesse McDonald, *Michelangelo* (London: PRC Publishing Ltd., 1990), 10.

4. Nerét, *Michelangelo*, 29.

5. The song "The Michelangelo Blues," by Rich Rubietta, tells the life story and work ethic of Michelangelo. Listen to the song on the CD *Room 4U & Me*, on www.CDBaby.com/Rubietta.

SENSATIONAL AFTER 60
CONTRIBUTORS

Jane Rubietta, international speaker and cofounder of Abounding Ministries, received her Bachelor of Science in Business and attended Trinity Divinity School in Illinois. She is the Assistant Director and Manuscript Coordinator for the Write-to-Publish Conference in Wheaton, Illinois. She is an award-winning author of 11 books, including *Quiet Places, Still Waters,* and *Come Along: The Journey into a More Intimate Faith.* For more information, visit www.janerubietta.com.

James Upchurch, M.D., GYN, graduated from the Medical College of Alabama. Following his four years of service in the United States Air Force, in which he assumed the position of Captain, Dr. Upchurch completed an OB-GYN residency and practiced for 32 years in Birmingham. His work has been published in several medical journals, including the American Journal of Obstetrics and Gynecology.

Dr. Debra K. Goodwin, Ph.D., R.D., is an Associate Professor and Department Head of Family & Consumer Sciences at Jacksonville State University in Alabama. She received a B.S. in Administrative Dietetics from Jacksonville State University, an M.A. in Allied Health Education from the University of Alabama, and a Ph.D. in Health Education and Health Promotion from the University of Alabama. Her research interests include adolescent nutrition, women's nutrition, and workplace wellness. She has given numerous presentations and published many articles on adolescent diabetes and menu modification. To contact Dr. Goodwin, e-mail her at dgoodwin@jsu.edu.

Photographer John Keith was born and raised in Washington, D.C., and graduated from the acclaimed photography program at Montgomery College. He owns his own photography business, which has grown a lot since its opening in 1984. Some of his clients include Lockheed Martin, IBM, the Republican National Committee, and Mercantile Bank. John is also a contributing photographer for *Frederick* magazine, of Frederick, Maryland. For more information, contact John at keithpix@msn.com or visit www.johnkeithphotography.com.

ABOUT THE AUTHOR

SHIRLEY W. MITCHELL

"The Golden Egg of Aging"

Shirley W. Mitchell, Dale Carnegie graduate and member of Toastmasters International, was awarded the 2004 Citizen of the Year Award by the Albertville Chamber of Commerce for her contributions to the betterment of society through local community projects. Her glowing smile won her the most Stunning Smile Award during the 2000 Ms. Senior Alabama pageant, and she won the 1997 Woman of Achievement Award, presented by the Albertville Business and Professional Women's Club. Shirley is basking in the time of her life, following biggest passions: writing, speaking, traveling, and being a mother, grandmother, and great-grandmother.

Shirley attended Dr. Ken Dychtwald's "Age Wave Institute" in New York and Dr. Walter M. Bortz II's seminar "Dare to be 100" in California. She also attends the annual Write-to-Publish Conference at Wheaton College. She has published multiple books, including *The Beauty of Being God's Woman*, *Spiritual Sparks for Busy Women*, and *Fabulous Aging Attitudes*.

Known today as The Golden Egg of Aging, Shirley is the owner of the syndicated media groups Fabulous After 50, Sensational After 60, and Aging Outside the Box. She is the columnist of the syndicated Fabulous After 50 online column, a featured columnist for *Senior Lifestyle Magazine*, writer of the *Passionate Sparks* online newsletter, and a member of The Lit Chicks Literary Writers Critique Group of Sand Mountain, Alabama.

Shirley is the celebrity radio talk show host of the syndicated radio shows *Aging Outside the Box* and *Christian Spiritual Sparks*.

Her passion is being fabulous at any age.

EXTEND THE IMPACT!

If your group or club is interested in booking Shirley W. Mitchell for an upcoming speaking event, conference, seminar, banquet, workshop, or retreat, please contact the Managing Agent-Producer at:

Lighthouse Coastal Productions
466 Sardis Cutoff Road
Sardis City, AL 35956
agent@lighthousecoastal.com
www.lighthousecoastal.com

www.fabulousafter50.com
www.sensationalafter60.com
www.agingoutsidethebox.net